Imprint

Impressum

Bibliografische Information der Deutschen Nationalbibliothek: Die Deutsche Nationalbibliothek verzeichnet diese Publikation in der Deutschen Nationalbibliografie; detaillierte bibliografische Daten sind im internet über www.dnd.de abrufbar.

Bibliographic information from the German National Library: The German National Library lists this publication in the German National Bibliography; detailed bibliographic data are available on the Internet at www.dnb.de.

Herstellung und Verlag: BoD - Books on Demand, Norderstedt

ISBN: 9783756212620

NO-POINT

ANDREAS MÜLLER
JUSTIN ALLEN

Acknowledgements from Andreas Müller:

Thanks to Nadine and Soham, Tony and Claire Parsons

Acknowledgements from Justin Allen:

Thanks to my family, close and far friends and Andreas

CONTENTS

Preface: March 31, 2022
PREFACE: JUSTIN ALLEN 11

Introduction: March 31, 2022
INTRODUCTION: ANDREAS MÜLLER 13

Talk 15: January 24, 2021
THISNESS 15

Talk 16: February 28, 2021
WHAT'S REALLY REAL? 45

Talk 17: April 21, 2021
I ROBOT 71

Talk 18: May 21, 2021
POST-LIFE 89

Talk 19: June 24, 2021
I WAS NEVER HAPPY BEING ME 117

Talk 20: July 21, 2021
EVEN THE MICROSCOPE CONFIRMS YOU'RE NOT THERE 157

Talk 21: December 21, 2021 (winter solstice)
PLACEBO 193

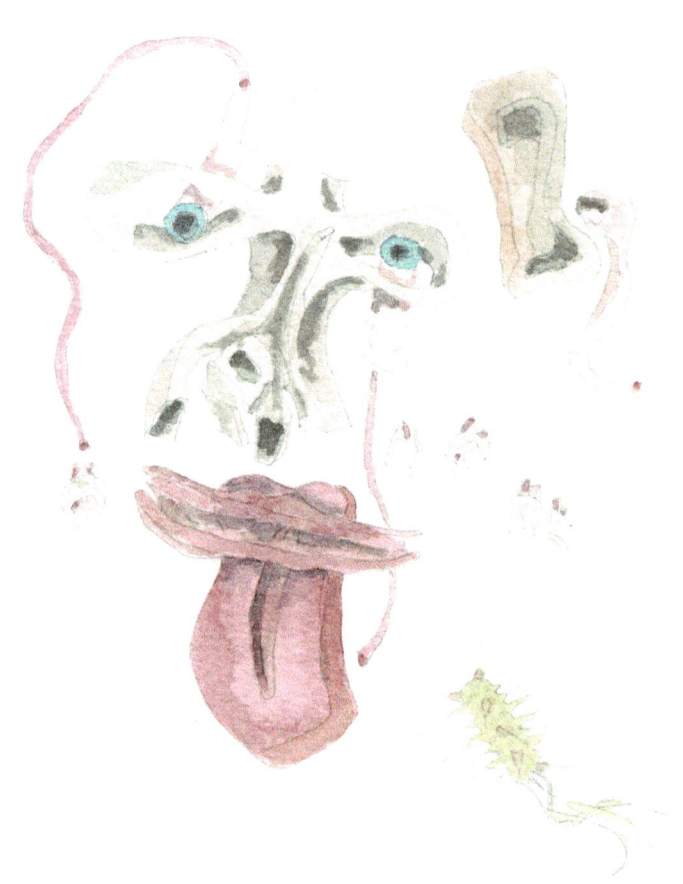

PREFACE

This is a continuation of talks about nothing between Andreas and myself. Again, there is no meaning and nothing to gain or learn from these 7 additional talks. Not that the talks from *No-Point Perspective (2020)* offered something, but this series offers even less; less talks, less pages and less paintings, but it may more tightly explore the topic of "no one" being there.

Our last talk from *No-Point Perspective (2020)* happened on March 23rd, 2020 and our first talk for *No-Point (2022)* took place on January 24th, 2021. Almost one year after our last talk from *NPP (2020)*, we started to talk again, for no clear or real reason, they just seemed to happen and were recorded and shared live and now transcribed. Having already covered teachers and gurus and various "misunderstandings" from our first set of talks, this series is possibly more relaxed and, dare I say, focused.

It is just incredibly enjoyable to talk about nothing with someone that also seems to enjoy talking about nothing. We have created a book that has essentially recorded "small-talk," with even less meaning than the dreaded conversation you may have with someone about the weather. This series of talks took place from January 24th, 2021 to December 21st, 2021.

INTRODUCTION

After having published *No-Point-Perspective* in 2020, there did not seem to be a point in making another book. We already covered a lot in the first book and seemed to have approached this (non-)issue from various angles. However, Justin and I had the energy to continue our conversations and so, 7 more talks happened. We slightly changed the format for these talks, as they were not done privately via Skype, but broadcasted online, so people could watch us talk in real-time. Of course, this may not make a difference for you as a reader.

I love that our conversations continued in spite of there being no-point to them. Enjoyable as before, covering other aspects here and there, these conversations are the very no-thing apparently happening through the talks transcribed in this book.

THISNESS

Andreas Müller:	Exactly. All right. I think that's about it regarding the explanation (laughing). I'm ready.
Justin Allen:	All right (both laughing). We don't have a plan but I did write a question before.
Andreas Müller:	All right.
Justin Allen:	So, in that sense, it's a little bit planned. (laughing)
Andreas Müller:	Okay. Well, when we talked two days ago, there was no plan.
Justin Allen:	Yeah (laughing). This is 30 minutes before this conversation plan.
Andreas Müller:	That's almost no plan.
Justin Allen:	Yeah. I wrote it down, but I'll be able to paraphrase it once I read it again. You start off a lot of times when you talk, you say, "So this is it." Right (waiting for confirmation)? And we could boil it down to that statement that this is it and this is all there is.
Justin Allen:	And what you're pointing to when you say this or a kind of logical question would be, "What do you mean by 'this'? What is 'this'"? And the way that I would try to paraphrase that, is that in this context, it would be the blue wall behind you and the

curtain, and the bed frame, yourself with the shirt (referring to the actual scene behind Andreas).

Justin Allen: And then the same going on here, a bookshelf behind me, our voices. And that's what "this" is. Yeah (waiting for confirmation)? And then to that, you would say that even though this is it, what I just described as "this," it's all apparent. It's apparently "this."

Andreas Müller: Yes. Yes.

Justin Allen: Yeah. So, it's apparently this. And then for the majority of us...

Andreas Müller: ... (laughing and waiting in excited expectation) ...

Justin Allen: No, but I'm saying something different now. For the majority of us, there's also what's happening in this "this," is an apparent "me."

Andreas Müller: Yes. One could say so. The illusion to be someone. Yes.

Justin Allen: Right. And that would also be part of the description of "this."

Andreas Müller: This would also be what seems to be happening. Absolutely. Yes.

Justin Allen: And then conversely, for the minority, there is an apparent "no me" happening.

Andreas Müller: There isn't anyone. Yeah. Well, you can't say that because it's not really "a happening," but yes, there isn't anyone there. Yes.

Justin Allen: Yeah. Or there's nothing happening.

Andreas Müller: Or not the illusion. Yeah.

Justin Allen: Okay. So, for the majority, there's the illusion apparently happening.

Andreas Müller: That's what seems to be happening.

Justin Allen: And that's part of the "this," the "thisness."

Andreas Müller: Absolutely. That's wholeness. Yes.

Justin Allen: And a "me" not happening, or an illusion of a "me" not happening is also a part of "this."

Andreas Müller: Yeah. It's not really a part of, but yes. That's also what seems to be happening. Exactly.

Justin Allen: When I put it that way, then for me at least, it really evens the playing field (both laughing). It just takes away any potential excitement. Kind of like how you might previously imagine or how it could be imagined, what you're talking about.

Andreas Müller: Exactly. Yes. What we speak about is very unexciting because it's all there is and it's natural in a way.

Justin Allen: The way that I just put it… in that context, at least for me, it makes it so (looking for the word flat) … It's not unique… It also doesn't feel as mysterious in a way because it's almost like nothing different is being said and there's no difference (laughing).

Andreas Müller: Well, in the end, that's what's constantly being said.

Justin Allen: Right.

Andreas Müller: There is no difference between anything and… Not as a teaching, but of course, there is no difference. And the illusion of "I am," that I'm "me" and I'm different, and Andreas is different from me, and wholeness is different from me is a complete illusion, of course.

Andreas Müller:	What's being pointed to is very ordinary and normal. The natural reality, so to speak, is normal. It's nothing special. The person, so to speak, might get excited about it with the idea of, "I will get that. It's great and I will have it. I will own it." That's the excitement basically.
Justin Allen:	Yeah. The potential for excitement. Yeah.
Andreas Müller:	Yeah. Exactly.
Justin Allen:	But it's really clear when you say, at least in that structure that I just put it in, saying that "this" is it, this is all there is, and part of... Maybe that's not the right word to use, but part of that description of "this" and this is it, is also the apparent "me's" that are apparently happening, and then the nothing happening or the non-illusion of a "me," which isn't happening but that's also in this description of "this."
Andreas Müller:	So to speak. Yes.
Justin Allen:	So then in that sense, automatically, there's no hierarchy, there's no separation, there's no one better than the other.
Andreas Müller:	Not a single bit. Absolutely. This is it exactly as it is. The person, of course, thinks that I want to show something that the person can see, "Ah, it's this," in order for "this" to make a difference.
Andreas Müller:	The person would hope, "When I get that, then there will be a difference." But no, that's not what is meant. It's exactly "this," exactly as it is. That's all there is, so to speak.
Justin Allen:	Yeah.
Andreas Müller:	Yeah. Yep.

Justin Allen:	Okay.
Andreas Müller:	That's why there is no message, so to speak. It's not saying this to anyone in order to create a difference.
Justin Allen:	Yeah. Because also, there can be no difference (laughing).
Andreas Müller:	It can't be. There just isn't. Yes. And the pointing to "this" doesn't make a difference either. The person is constantly complaining about that, "Nothing changes. I'm listening to this and nothing happens..." (laughing). Yes, there is no change really.
Justin Allen:	Yeah.
Andreas Müller:	Or difference.
Justin Allen:	Okay. And the next thing is... I guess this is similar to what we just talked about, but it's put a different way. I wrote, "As obvious as it is that someone is there... (pause)"
Justin Allen:	If you have these kinds of conversations, and we mentioned this in the book (referring to *No-Point Perspective*), but it's so obvious that there's someone there for the majority of the people.
Andreas Müller:	Yes.
Justin Allen:	When they try to define themselves or to define what it is (what they are), you (they or someone) can't really do it, but your final sentence if you've been questioned to answer, "What are you?" You just say, "Well, it's just obvious that I'm there. It's so obvious. It's natural." (What a typical answer is)
Justin Allen:	And then you (someone) might give reasons. You say, "Well, it's obvious that I'm there because I'm

here hearing myself talk and I'm emitting words and I know what happened yesterday and one minute ago." But you (they or someone) can't really pinpoint what you (actually) are or what it is that you (actually) are. You just know that you "are."

Andreas Müller: Yes. Exactly. Yes.

Justin Allen: And then the same as, at least how I've heard you talk about what it's like over there (referring to Andreas on the other side of the Zoom meeting) for you is that it's also obvious (laughing) that there's "no one" there.

Andreas Müller: Well, yeah. I sometimes say that, but not really.

Justin Allen: I'm not trying to trap you... where you say...

Andreas Müller: Yeah. I understand. Yeah. It's just the word "obviousness" doesn't really fit there anymore because the person would imply obviousness exactly with this knowing "I am," with this kind of awareness thing. And in that sense, there is no obviousness that there isn't anyone. There just isn't anyone.

Justin Allen: But it's not just been said by you. It's been said by the other people that are pointing to this topic, pointing to this "nothingness." Because you get questioned a lot about what it's like for you or what happened to you.

Justin Allen: For you, it's like the story of "me" and then there's nothing after that point. But then trying to explain... when you try to describe it or explain it, it's just obvious. A sentence that you might say is that it's obvious that there's "no one" there.

Andreas Müller: Yes.

Justin Allen:	It's just natural.
Andreas Müller:	It's natural. That's what this description of "obvious" tries to say.
Justin Allen:	But that's not so dissimilar to the... It's dissimilar in the sense, if I were to say (crosstalk)...
Andreas Müller:	I know. Oh, yeah. Oh, yes, absolutely.
Justin Allen:	One could say, "It's obvious that I'm here." The one difference is that it's obvious for the experience of a "me" where I'm saying it's obvious, but aside from that, it's also just... Even without the experience of a "me," it's how I would say it's just natural that I'm here. It's natural that there's an "I" that I refer to and the sense of "me" that I would refer to.
Andreas Müller:	Yeah.
Justin Allen:	And I feel like you can switch it around and say that's how you would have to always describe it. You'd still have to... It'd be different because there wouldn't be a "me" there that it's obvious for. But still, it's obvious and natural.
Andreas Müller:	Yeah. I understand. Yeah. In a way, both are the natural reality. One can't really say that one is natural and one isn't. It's actually exactly what we talked about in the beginning. Both just is what seems to be happening.
Justin Allen:	Right.
Andreas Müller:	Absolutely.
Justin Allen:	For me, I don't know why I was thinking about this but I was just thinking about how... If people speak about enlightenment from, let's say the spiritual or religious frame of reference (laughing), then they might say that it became clear that there was just

"awareness" or they would say that there was an "enlightenment," … "There was a moment and I became one or one with something, or I just wasn't there anymore or something."

Justin Allen: And they would say that it was an experience and it was an obvious experience, and it was a shift or a change.

Andreas Müller: There was a change. Exactly.

Justin Allen: Yeah.

Andreas Müller: Yes. Yeah, absolutely.

Justin Allen: And then they would say, "And then 'this' became the new point of view or the new perspective or the new…"

Andreas Müller: Truth. The new experience. The new reality for them, so to speak. Yeah.

Justin Allen: And for me, I get more… Based on what I just said or what we just talked about is that there isn't a change and it just stays natural. So just like how it's obvious… Like for you, there's not a change.

Andreas Müller: Yes, absolutely. Yes.

Justin Allen: And there can't be. By the way that you're describing this, there can't be a change because there was "no one" there ever in the first place to have transformed or changed into something else.

Andreas Müller: Yes, absolutely.

Justin Allen: And that's why, to me, just like this sense of, if you say the "me" and then take the "no me," … It's natural in both cases and it's obvious in both cases.

Andreas Müller: Yes. One could say so. Oh, absolutely. Yes.

Justin Allen: And that is also part of the kind of un-excitement of it or the extraordinary ordinariness of it, is that it all just stays and remains obvious (laughing).

Andreas Müller: Oh, absolutely. In a way, the claim saying, "Well, I'm still 'me,' I'm still a seeker, so to speak," is as much an honest report as saying, "Well, there is no one." In that sense, again, both is natural and both are the same. Absolutely. It's (crosstalk) what it is, an illusion, because there never really is anyone. But yeah.

Justin Allen: And both are obvious in both cases.

Andreas Müller: Yeah. You can't really compare those because the obviousness that the person would speak of is an awareness, describing a circumstance. And there being "no one" is not really a circumstance, it's not the opposite of being someone.

Justin Allen: Yeah.

Andreas Müller: So when I speak of obvious, actually, I also try to take it back immediately because obviousness immediately is somehow mixed up with being aware of. And in the end, I'm not running around in some kind of obviousness. In the end, there actually is no obviousness.

Justin Allen: But it seems similar to the experience of a "me" … It seems like, fundamentally, you can talk about how it's obvious that "I am" or that there's a "me," but when you talk about it, that's where it becomes a little bit like you give cause and effect or you say it's obvious because of this reason.

Andreas Müller: Yes, of course. But the person lives just in this reality.

Justin Allen:	Yeah. It's natural that they're there or at least that that sense is there.
Andreas Müller:	Yeah. Of course.
Justin Allen:	They couldn't describe it any better than you. Really, a person, an apparent person trying to describe themselves is just as failing as you trying to describe...
Andreas Müller:	Oh, of course. But the person wouldn't notice really. The person would somehow still believe there is "someone," and this "someone" is somehow knowable or experienceable.
Andreas Müller:	But yes, I know what you mean. Practically, they would fail. They would tell their name and who they are. In the end, they'd end up saying, "Well, I'm pure awareness, but I don't know what this actually is," which is one of those spiritual teachings. And they say what you are is pure awareness, but they also admit that you don't know what this actually is.
Justin Allen:	Yeah.
Andreas Müller:	But in their teaching, this doesn't count for very much.
Justin Allen:	But even outside of the teaching or a teacher, that (natural) obviousness of there being an "I," it's kind of like when you try to talk about the sense of "me" as a "me", you can't do it. You fail at it.
Andreas Müller:	Absolutely. Oh, absolutely. That's the thing. Knowing oneself is an illusion. No one knows themselves.
Justin Allen:	Right.
Andreas Müller:	And in a funny way, as you say, when the person tries to describe itself, it may even come to the

point that it can't really do it but it would still be from a separate perspective. But yes, knowing oneself is a dream. No one knows themselves.

Justin Allen: But that's kind of what I'm trying to get at, is that because it's so obvious, it's equally obvious to the "me" that they're there, but also that they're not there or that there's not something. No (seeing the expression of Andreas)?

Andreas Müller: No. Because for the person, there's only presence. And the rest would be already conclusions, understanding, noticing. But it would never really... Even in the noticing that it can't know itself, the person would somehow confirm itself.

Justin Allen: And let's say that it apparently happens that this person really can no longer confirm themselves, where they can't even say, "I'm not there anymore." Because that's just not something that they can rely on anymore that there's an "I" there to even say that they're there or not.

Andreas Müller: Well, this would just be the melting away of the separate energy, but it wouldn't...

Justin Allen: But that's what I mean. That's what I'm trying to say is that imagine that there was a "me" and the "me" started to go, "Is there a 'me'"? What is this "me"? And it feels so obvious that they're there, but at the same time, it starts to feel "obvious" that they're not there.

Andreas Müller: Yes. This can happen. Yes. Yes.

Justin Allen: And that is such a... (crosstalk) ...

Andreas Müller: (crosstalk) ... half-dead or half-alive then.

Justin Allen: Yeah. But they're still the same. You know what I mean?

Andreas Müller:	Oh. It would just be what apparently happens. Absolutely. It would be...
Justin Allen:	Let's say that you did... for lack of a better word... this isn't the right way to say it, but that you transition from an apparent "me" to a "no me."
Andreas Müller:	Yeah. Fade out. That's basically my story. This would be my story in the end.
Justin Allen:	Yeah. But the fade-out would be so natural, it wouldn't be a change. You know what I mean? It would just be the exact same obviousness of... The reality of the "me" is it's unknowable, even for a "me" or a "no me."
Andreas Müller:	Oh, yeah. Absolutely. It is natural. The illusion to be someone is natural and the end of that is natural too. Nothing changes in them.
Justin Allen:	Right. But nothing changes also because even as convinced as you (someone) are that you're there, (crosstalk)...
Andreas Müller:	You don't know it. Oh, absolutely. Oh, totally (laughing). Totally. That's what I mean, that someone knows themselves is an illusion. It never happened. Let's say through your whole life, you never knew who you are and that you are and what you are. So, yes, this will not change. Exactly. One could say that how it was all the time will not change.
Justin Allen:	Right.
Andreas Müller:	But this isn't really logical because, of course, from the sense of the person, there is constantly this illusion. As you say, seen from the person, one's own presence is so natural, you don't even really think about that.

Justin Allen:	Yeah.
Andreas Müller:	Even when you're working with those concepts of "me," "no me," it's so natural that "I am" and that I'm on a path and that this is my life, and that "me"/ "no me" is what I'm interested in and all, but nothing changes. Absolutely.
Justin Allen:	And what's artificial in that? ... If it's just natural that you're not there, then the artificial is? ... the explaining and the describing of how you are there?
Andreas Müller:	Well, artificial is a story because nothing's really artificial in that sense.
Justin Allen:	That's the story. If you were to say, "I'm here because when I look at my photos from 10 years ago, I see a difference and I have memories that verify that there's been this change, and that I've been witness to the changing," that's artificial.
Andreas Müller:	Well, no, the assumption that there really is someone who experiences all of that.
Justin Allen:	Yeah. To experience that is artificial... You're already explaining...
Andreas Müller:	Something that doesn't happen, that doesn't have any reality.
Justin Allen:	Right.
Andreas Müller:	Yes. Yeah.
Justin Allen:	I think that's a better word to use is artificial than... What's the word, the other option? Illusion.
Andreas Müller:	Yeah.
Justin Allen:	I like artificial better than illusion.

Andreas Müller:	Yeah. Yeah. Illusion has this connotation in a way. It's also the spiritual connotation. And it still sounds as if there is something in a way.
Justin Allen:	But artificial would be a good alternative.
Andreas Müller:	Yeah. But it's (crosstalk) description, I think, because artificial has this negative connotation. No one wants artificial in a way (laughing). Artificial has a bad reputation.
Justin Allen:	Yeah. But it would be a good alternative word as far as they can be used in the same context.
Andreas Müller:	Yeah. I do sometimes.
Justin Allen:	I just wanted to say, what you mean by artificial is artificial is the illusion and the illusion is the... Generally, the illusion is the dream and the dream is that I'm there. And when you say, "I'm there," that comes from trying to describe or understand or know this obviousness, which is, in this case...
Andreas Müller:	Well, it's just an experience. The person would just experience itself and say, "Well, I'm here. I am." And yes, it immediately seems like a circumstance that's known. I am.
Justin Allen:	Yeah. You don't just say, "I am." Right? You say, "I am," generally, then you're giving reasons why you are.
Andreas Müller:	Yeah. That comes afterwards. Actually, I would say there can be this sense of "I am" without any kind of processing, at least for moments, for a while, and then comes the processing. And pretty quickly, you end up telling yourself a whole story about the world.
Justin Allen:	Yeah. And that would be the illusion and the artificialness of that person's...

Andreas Müller:	Yes, it's actually this first sense of presence which would be artificial.
Justin Allen:	Then the other things you're just saying are?
Andreas Müller:	Apparently artificial. That's the thing.
Justin Allen:	Well, the first thing's apparently artificial.
Andreas Müller:	Again.
Justin Allen:	The first sense of "I am" is artificial.
Andreas Müller:	Yes. But as a description. Yeah, absolutely. Yep.
Justin Allen:	That's an interesting point for me now, that the very initial illusion or the initial artificial moment is the "I am" sense.
Andreas Müller:	Sense. Not the story. Yeah. Actually, that's already information from the brain when you tell the story. Well, "I am," that's already processed. That's actually already the sense of presence processed in the story.
Justin Allen:	Right. So let's just call the very first thing a sense.
Andreas Müller:	Yeah.
Justin Allen:	Then the second thing is the story (both laughing).
Andreas Müller:	Yes. And the story gets more and more...
Justin Allen:	Multiplied. The story gets multiplied.
Andreas Müller:	Yes.
Justin Allen:	Yeah. Okay. So the first thing is, as soon as there's a sensed "I" or a sensed "me," that's the first or that's the initial illusion or that's the illusion.

Andreas Müller:	Well, it's an apparent illusion.
Justin Allen:	That's the apparent illusion and the apparent artificial beginning.
Andreas Müller:	Yes.
Justin Allen:	And then following that comes, exponentially, the story.
Andreas Müller:	Yeah. One could say so. Yeah.
Justin Allen:	The story, by nature of its foundation, its foundation being an illusion, then the story is also an illusion just because of that. Okay.
Andreas Müller:	Exactly. As this first sense of presence is illusory, everything that seems to come out of that or circle around the sense of presence is just as illusory as the sense of presence.
Justin Allen:	So then, for a "me" that's had that sense, that initial sense, "I am," and then goes about a life, and then the life creates 20 or 40 years of illusory stories.
Andreas Müller:	Yes (laughing). Yes.
Justin Allen:	And then there's somebody (laughing)...
Andreas Müller:	(laughing) ...years of believing some stuff. Yeah.
Justin Allen:	Yeah. And then if there's a moment, and using you as an example, if there's a case where the illusion dies, right, the illusion stops, and the illusion stops because that initial illusion of "I am" is no longer there.
Andreas Müller:	Yes.
Justin Allen:	That sense, "I am," is gone.

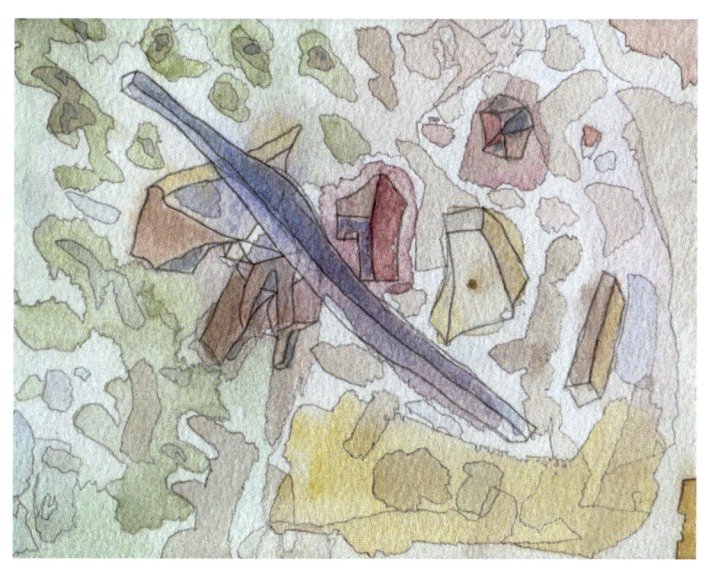

Andreas Müller:	Yes.
Justin Allen:	Then from that point on, your life goes on for another 20 or 40 years with things happening identically to the other people in the sense that life still is happening.
Andreas Müller:	So to speak.
Justin Allen:	You have a family and...
Andreas Müller:	There's food and waking up in the morning and going to bed at night.
Justin Allen:	But there's no more illusion happening because there is no longer that initial illusion of "I am."
Andreas Müller:	Exactly. There is no waking up anymore. There is no coming into presence anymore. Yeah. Yep. (Both laughing) What we were just describing was life and death (laughing). The apparent birth, then you have a life full of stories and realities, and then it just drops and it's over.
Justin Allen:	And there's no apparent difference between your case and somebody else's case in the sense that life is also still happening for them the exact same way as it's happening to you.
Andreas Müller:	Yes and no, because one can't really separate that. In a way, yes, and in a way, no. Because when there is the sense of "I am," life seems to be circled around this "I am" and life seems to be about finding fulfillment. You can't really separate it. You know what I mean?
Justin Allen:	Yeah.
Andreas Müller:	It's not the same because there is no attempt to fulfill myself anymore, there is no reading books in

order to find an answer. There is just no seeking anymore.

Andreas Müller: And somehow, apparently, life is according to that. But you can't just separate life. But in a way, both would be still the same. Both would still be what seems to be happening.

Justin Allen: Right. Because when you give your talks...

Andreas Müller: One more sentence. But the person, of course, seeing me how I live, the person would just say, "Well, that's very ordinary and not special at all. Maybe even boring."

Justin Allen: Yeah. You're not living up to their expectations (laughing).

Andreas Müller: Not so far (laughing).

Justin Allen: But when you're giving your talks, you're there talking to an audience of, maybe 10 people. And assuming that there's apparent illusory "I am's" happening for those 10 people, there's no difference in the sense that you're all there in the same space.

Andreas Müller: Oh, it's all wholeness. Absolutely. It would just be an illusion that it's otherwise. Oh, absolutely. That's why there is never anything to reach or to attain. Not a single bit. It would just be part of an illusion, but it's not happening. No one is different. No one is separate. Absolutely. A hundred percent. Yeah.

Justin Allen: And when you go about your life, for example, you still say the words, "I believe."

Andreas Müller: Sometimes. Yeah.

Justin Allen: You probably don't do it in the context of these talks, but I'm sure when you're at home and you say something like, "Yeah, I believe that's the right answer." (laughing)

Andreas Müller: Yeah. Oh, yeah, absolutely. Oh, yeah, of course. Why not? Yeah.

Justin Allen: So that's what I mean in the sense that you still go about life with belief, not beliefs like, "This is going to fulfill me and end my search," because there's no longer a search, but there still is a belief in the sense, when you turn the TV on, you believe...

Justin Allen: Or when you take your remote and you press the on button, you believe that (laughing) your TV's going to turn on (laughing). You're going about your life in a totally... Almost un-different way as beforehand.

Andreas Müller: Oh, absolutely. Oh, totally. Yeah. Just the assumption dropped that at some point in the future, it will be different. No, it'll never be different. This dream dropped that it can be different.

Andreas Müller: Absolutely. Totally. In that sense, there is nothing else than ordinary living, whatever that is. It's not that there is someone who knows what that means, but of course. Yeah.

Justin Allen: Talking about it in this way then, and I guess maybe this is the case for you, is that when the apparent illusion of you being there was no longer there, then for me, hearing this and the way that we've been talking about it, it means that it must have been very un-shocking (unspectacular).

Andreas Müller: Yes. One could almost say so. Yes. It was a bit unexpected. It is unexpected that there is nothing else to find and that there is no change. But as we said, on the other hand, it's very natural and ordinary.

Justin Allen:	It also sounds like it might have been almost unclear or unobvious that there is a "no me" because it seems so natural and so...
Andreas Müller:	Yes, but this is completely ... so when the person dies, so to speak, this isn't really what the focus is on. The ending point, so to speak, was not, "Oh, I died. Oh, finally, it happened. Oh, cool, the 'I' died. That's it. That's what I wanted." No. There was just no seeking anymore and everything was totally fine.
Justin Allen:	Right. And that's what I mean. And that event, it's a little bit... I'm interested in dispelling the (myth)... I'm sure you've probably done this a lot in your talks and we also talked about this, but there's not some grand, obvious, "Oh my God." (Referring here to some kind of epiphany)
Andreas Müller:	Can be. For some people, there can be an event. What we are talking about is this fading away. So in the story, there can also be an event, but it would still be ordinary.
Justin Allen:	That's what I mean. Even if there were an event, then that change would be, there's "no one" there, so how could there be such an excitable moment? You know what I mean? Because there'd be no one there to even...
Andreas Müller:	Yes, this is not logical, this message is not logical.
Justin Allen:	No, but in your case then, the way that you described it is that it seems like it almost would've been... I can only do this in the context of a "me" perspective, of an "I am" perspective.
Justin Allen:	But if it were happening and then the "me" dropped away, so to speak, or it was fading out as in your case, maybe the questions would be,

	"What's the difference? Am I here anymore or did it happen to me"?
Andreas Müller:	Yeah. But...
Justin Allen:	If you don't notice any big... (change, because change doesn't really happen)
Andreas Müller:	Yeah. Absolutely. Oh, yeah. I had this question or my brain was able to come up with that question, of course.
Justin Allen:	Yeah.
Andreas Müller:	But I didn't get any answer (laughing). Is it this now? But there wasn't an answer coming back. But yeah, of course. Yeah.
Justin Allen:	Yeah. That's what I think is remarkable... I know you speak about it a lot and I've heard it spoken by others, is the ordinariness of it or the... Obvious is the other word, but the ordinariness of it.
Andreas Müller:	Yeah. I mean, the natural reality, what's being apparently described with "this is it," it's whole and complete, and all those things is the natural reality and it's ordinary. It's not ordinary in a sense that the person would regard ordinary.
Andreas Müller:	For the person, ordinary would be, "Well, I know it. It's this old stuff from this... Well, I've experienced this 100 million times, that's why it's ordinary."
Justin Allen:	Yeah.
Andreas Müller:	It's ordinary on the one hand, what we speak about, but it's not coming from a known experience. In that sense, it's not really ordinary, but yes. Again, can't be explained. It's just ordinary.

Andreas Müller:	Well, ordinary is another word that no one knows really what ordinary is. In a way, it's just ordinary in contrast to the person's ideas of what fulfillment would look like. And that's definitely not ordinary.
Justin Allen:	You mean generally, people's expectations or ideas of what... (referring to what people think, enlightenment or awakening or total fulfillment would be like)
Andreas Müller:	Exactly. Exactly.
Justin Allen:	Yeah.
Andreas Müller:	In contrast to those ideas and expectations, what we speak about is ordinary because it's this. It's sitting in front of a screen, it's breathing, it's getting up in the morning. It's those things.
Andreas Müller:	But it's not ordinary... That's the difficult thing with the ordinary. For the person, as I said, ordinary would be known. And in a way, this ordinariness is what the person wants to escape from into something that's special and gorgeous and great and wow.
Justin Allen:	Yeah. To put this in the context of spirituality then, I've read and heard often about how there's got to be some kind of 'koan' or some kind of quotable sentence from all of them about how it's right there in front of your face and you don't see it. Something like that.
Justin Allen:	And they're alluding to how... If they elaborate on that, then they allude to how it's just so strikingly obvious talking about enlightenment or whatever. I know that it's not what you mean.
Andreas Müller:	Yeah. Exactly. This story would also apply to the recognition that I'm pure awareness.

Justin Allen:	Yeah.
Andreas Müller:	This can also come about like, "Well, it's so obvious." So they could apply this story also to the personal experience of, "I'm pure awareness," or something.
Justin Allen:	But they're using it to say that it's so obvious.
Andreas Müller:	Yeah.
Justin Allen:	It's right there. They use the examples of how you can't find your key but it's on your neck.
Andreas Müller:	Yeah. Exactly. Yeah.
Justin Allen:	Something like that.
Andreas Müller:	But I hardly say that, actually. You'll hardly hear me say something about, "It's so obvious."
Justin Allen:	Oh, no. You don't say it.
Andreas Müller:	Yeah. Thank you. I don't.
Justin Allen:	I'm saying in the spiritual context, they say that.
Andreas Müller:	Yeah. They say it. Yeah.
Justin Allen:	How the listener hears it is they can relate to that because they've experienced, in their own life, moments how they're searching for something so hard but it's right there in front of them and it's because they're searching so hard that they can't see it.
Andreas Müller:	Yeah.
Justin Allen:	So the teaching for them is always like, just let go and relax and then you'll see it.

Andreas Müller:	Yeah. Yes.
Justin Allen:	But in your context, it's not that you say that, but it's... Or in the spiritual context, they're also saying that it's so obvious, this enlightenment or whatever, that that's what makes it so hard to attain because the way that the brain is trained or the way that you're conditioned is to constantly look for it. And then looking for it just perpetuates the search forever.
Andreas Müller:	Yeah.
Justin Allen:	And that's relatable in a way to when you bring this topic of obviousness and searching into your context.
Andreas Müller:	Yeah.
Justin Allen:	Just only in the sense that, for you, it's obvious that there's "no one" there, there's nothing there, there never was. And for the person, if it's an illusion and that very initial illusion is "I am," which is just an illusion, then it is also so obvious that that's never been the case and that they're not there. You're never saying that this is what you need to do.
Andreas Müller:	No. I don't do that.
Justin Allen:	But you're pointing to the obvious nature of there is "no one" there.
Andreas Müller:	Yeah, if you want so, apparently. It's an apparent pointing. That's the thing. Pointing is too much actually already. But yeah (Justin laughing). The thing is, I think it's just hard to compare me, so to speak, with those.
Andreas Müller:	You can't really compare a personal teaching with what's being said here because, on the one hand, one would always compare differences.

Justin Allen:	Yeah. I guess I'm not trying to compare it, but I'm more interested... From the very first five minutes of our talk, we talked about how when the "me," or at least in your case, when the "me" faded away that it was questionable in the sense that it wasn't from night to day immediately, that there was this fading out and that you could question it and say... At least the questions could arise kind of like, "Is this it? Can this be it...(crosstalk)"?
Andreas Müller:	Yeah, absolutely. Totally. I had this. Oh, yeah.
Justin Allen:	It's so unexciting. It's so uneventful. How can it be...
Andreas Müller:	Yes.
Justin Allen:	And you could imagine how just that train of thoughts, that you were about to fade out, it could bring you back to life with a whole series of new questions about how it can't be this because it's got to be this... (something more interesting or exciting or amazing)
Andreas Müller:	Not really, because then it's not fading out. That's the thing. Either it's fading out or not.
Justin Allen:	That's what you can say now. That's what you can say now, but before... (both laughing)
Andreas Müller:	(Andreas laughing)
Justin Allen:	My only interest is in that specific naturalness about how... Then I can relate it to spirituality. And maybe not all the spirituality is a teaching. Some of it might not be. It might just be...
Andreas Müller:	Well, now it's about words, but I would call every teaching (in this context) spirituality. But of course, they...

Justin Allen:	Yeah, but I mean, for example, you don't know what Buddha really was or meant...
Andreas Müller:	Yeah. That's true.
Justin Allen:	... alluding to. And I'm just saying...
Andreas Müller:	Oh, yeah, of course. Yeah.
Justin Allen:	They could have been talking about. (This message)
Andreas Müller:	Absolutely. Absolutely. Yeah.
Justin Allen:	So those sentences, those original sentences about how it's so obvious, maybe somebody says, "It's right in front of your face. You're missing it." That's the exact same thing as saying, "You're not there. It's so obvious."
Andreas Müller:	Absolutely. It's never the sentences. It's never the words. And of course, if someone said something 2,000 years ago, "It's all wholeness," you'd just have no idea what was meant or not.
Justin Allen:	So that's why I'm just trying to put that... I'm not trying to put a teacher into this context. I'm just talking about how people have read several books; they've probably come upon somebody that said this sentence.
Justin Allen:	And how I can imagine it being relatable in a way about what we were just talking about, how the fading away is so... It's just a natural thing. Then it's just obvious, "Ah, I'm not there anymore." It's not obvious as a point of view for somebody, but it's just like, kind of in a quotation, the new natural, which isn't really different.
Justin Allen:	Then that would be a way to generate the sentence, "It's so obvious, you just can't see it." It's the same

way as when you're talking to these people, you can't address them as a "me."

Andreas Müller: Yes. Impossible.

Justin Allen: But you still have to call their name and you still look when somebody says, "Andreas."

Andreas Müller: Yeah. But that's just happening. Yeah.

Justin Allen: That's what I mean, is that it's still so...

Andreas Müller: No way out.

Justin Allen: Yeah.

Andreas Müller: Yeah. Yeah.

Justin Allen: Again, that would be a way to generate that sentence would be because it's almost like you can say to everybody... You would have to say to everybody, "You're not there. You just think you are."

Andreas Müller: No. Not really. No, because it's not coming from an obviousness. That's the thing. There isn't anyone and there is no need from my side to clarify that up because it's not a known circumstance. It is not a circumstance that I live in that, actually, everyone should know before.

Justin Allen: No, I'm not saying that you would say that people should know it, but from your point of view, if somebody's talking to themselves and referring to themselves and it's obvious that, for them - there is a "me" happening...

Andreas Müller: Yes.

Justin Allen: For you, you're still talking to them and there's not a "me" there happening for them.

Andreas Müller: Yeah (laughing). All right. It's already 50 minutes.

Justin Allen: All right. Good. I've run out of things to say. (Both laughing)

WHAT'S REALLY REAL?

Andreas Müller:	We're recording. Hello and welcome. Hi Justin. Nice to see you.
Justin Allen:	Nice to see you too.
Andreas Müller:	Do we have an agenda?
Justin Allen:	No, we don't have an agenda.
Andreas Müller:	No? All right.
Justin Allen:	Before these talks, there's always a potential agenda, where I have some ideas of what to talk about, but then I don't take notes. I'm like a bad comedian (laughing), a good comedian will have an idea for a joke that just pops in and then they'll write it down as a note and maybe work on it later. I'm not doing that.
Andreas Müller:	Yeah. Sounds good. (laughing)
Justin Allen:	Then I'm left, one minute before the Zoom meeting, a little bit anxious because maybe I don't have anything to talk about.
Andreas Müller:	Yeah. Yeah.
Justin Allen:	And I was thinking there's a natural way that I can imagine starting this off. And then I think, well, maybe it's repetitive, but that's the only way to do it.

	So I could imagine that this is repeating last week, but then I've listened to enough of your Zoom talks to know that repetition isn't a... (laughing)
Andreas Müller:	A problem? (laughing)
Justin Allen:	... isn't an apparent dissuasion.
Andreas Müller:	Yes. I mean, apparently, it seems to be repetitive, but it actually isn't.
Justin Allen:	Yeah. (laughing)
Andreas Müller:	Kind of fresh, like every sunset, so to speak, isn't really repetitive. It's just what seems to be happening, but not really again and again and again.
Justin Allen:	For me, the most natural way to start off right now is to point things out. So by pointing out, I mean, I like to start off saying that the red mug that you're drinking out of right now, and the blue shirt that you're wearing and all the background behind you, is in a sense, "real." And that, I just mean the objects that are all around us are really there, let's say. And that in this composition of objects and things that are happening, you and me and all the guests here, the only thing that isn't happening in this kind of reality is a "me" or the sense of experiencing and the sense of somebody or something being there. To me, condensing the point of these talks or the message is really saying that experience is the thing that's not actually happening or experience is the only real illusion, or let's say the fundamental illusion, which then makes things like all the objects behind you seem real and that they're really there.
Andreas Müller:	That's the thing. On the one hand, this could be the message, so to speak, saying, yes, there is "no one," and everything else is real, but on the other

hand, when there is "no one," it would exactly be this statement, which wouldn't be possible anymore. Because when there isn't anyone, there isn't anyone able to make this statement saying the carpet, the wall and the shirt is real. But in a way it is like that.

Justin Allen: So the direct message though... if we're trying to make it as basic, superficially, as basic as possible, it's the experiencer or experience is the real fundamental illusion and the message isn't really focused on all the objects that are around it. Maybe it's a concession in a way to not talk about the objects, because if you start saying nothing's real, which is what you do ultimately say at some point, it's maybe a little bit more confusing, because the focus is more on the experience first.

Andreas Müller: Yeah. In a way, one could say so. I mean, there is "no one" and the rest is just automatic. In the end, you don't even need to talk about that because there is "no one," there's absolutely no need also to talk about objects being real or unreal or about all the stuff surrounding the apparent it. Because when there is "no one," all the other things just drop automatically.

Justin Allen: Right.

Andreas Müller: So if there would be a question, not that there is one, but the question would only be if there's someone or not, because when there is someone, the whole dream happens and if there isn't, everything else drops within.

Justin Allen: And for that sensed, that illusory sensed experience, that seems to be happening to all these people... I don't mean on the Zoom call (laughing). I just mean in general, all the people. That's the focus. I mean, that's the interest for them in general. They're not really interested in, are these objects real or not real? Ultimately, they're questioning everything about themselves. And ultimately the question always is "them," it's what's happening to "me" or how do I get rid of "me" or what do I do with "me" or how do I improve "me" or whatever.

Andreas Müller: So it's absolutely about objects. For the person, it's totally about the objects, all the time, seeing itself as an object and everything else as an objectified world. So it's constantly about objects for the person.

Justin Allen: Yeah. But not objects in the conventional sense.

Andreas Müller: I know.

Justin Allen: Yeah. But now when you say that, then I have to point out or I feel like I need to point out, objects to you in this sense would also mean a thought is an object.

Andreas Müller: Yes, absolutely.

Justin Allen: All right. And then my identity is an object and a feeling would be an object and an emotion would be an object.

Andreas Müller: That's how the person would regard it. Exactly. Yes.

Justin Allen: But I'm saying that if we try to eliminate the objects from the conversation, then it falls only onto the sense of experience.

Andreas Müller: Yeah.

Justin Allen: From what your message is saying, that's the fundamental illusion.

Andreas Müller: If you would say that there is an illusion, yes. Totally. Of course.

Justin Allen:	But that's the only illusion. (laughing)
Andreas Müller:	Yeah, absolutely. Oh yeah, of course. Totally.
Justin Allen:	You could say all the other illusions happen because of this illusion (the illusion of experience).
Andreas Müller:	Well, the illusion that things are things, or that objects are really objects only happen for the experiencer. Yes, absolutely.
Justin Allen:	And what I'm saying is that... Let's say that there is such a thing as hierarchy and fundamental... (laughing)
Andreas Müller:	Yes. In the hierarchy of illusions. (laughing)
Justin Allen:	Yeah. And a starting point...
Andreas Müller:	Would be number one ("me").
Justin Allen:	And a starting point and an ending point or... Then the number one illusion is just that sensed experience of "I am."
Andreas Müller:	Absolutely. Only. As you said, in the end, it's the only illusion.
Justin Allen:	Yeah. And I like to talk about this right now or point this out because for me, when I was talking to you in the beginning (referring to the talks from *No-Point Perspective*) and before, when maybe I read a philosophy book or a spirituality book or a religious book or whatever, everything that I read, I would say I was, regardless of what the intention of the message was or the meaning or the teaching or whatever, I'm positive, I was totally reinterpreting it in some agenda that I had formed.
Andreas Müller:	Absolutely.

Justin Allen:	And that's basically unavoidable and there's nothing "you" can do about it. But then when I started to talk to you and we have a chronology of our talks (again referring to the talks from *No-Point Perspective*) and it's interesting, not that I have really gone to the book yet and looked through it since we published it. Of course, when I edited the talks, I read through it again and I would see how I was understanding the message in chapter one as compared to chapter five, let's say. And not that you can see a change, but I can definitely point out that I didn't get it at all that this message was about that (laughing), was about not being there. And you can see how many ways... I could even see the aha-moment, maybe if I looked at chapter four, I would think, "Ah, okay, I get it." But I could still see that even when I said I get it, I didn't get it. (laughing)
Andreas Müller:	The same would happen to the "me" in chapter eight and chapter 12.
Justin Allen:	Well, you're saying that the same would happen in every chapter because you can't get it. But you still can get the message differently. I'm not saying you can get it like...
Andreas Müller:	Oh yeah, of course. In a way, the person can always seemingly understand another aspect.
Justin Allen:	Yeah. Or at least even understand ... Let's just say that right now I started off this talk saying there's the objects behind you, there's you, there's thoughts happening. There's all the people. And generally, everybody could relate to all that, like yeah, those things are all happening. And then there could be another understanding where they say, "But maybe it's an illusion happening." But then if it was an illusion happening, they would be ignoring the fact that illusion is still happening to something (meaning the "me"). And they would never really

grasp that what's being pointed to, or really talked about is that that sensed experience or that sense (of "me") ... I think the best way to say it for me is sensed experience or the sense of experiencing.

Andreas Müller: Yeah.

Justin Allen: That's the thing being questioned in a way, or that's the thing that's being pointed to as the illusion.

Andreas Müller: Yes.

Justin Allen: And I'm positive, even as I'm saying this right now, and it's clear to me, I'm positive that there's a very good possibility that nobody's getting that it's really just about that. (laughing)

Andreas Müller: Well, yes, because in the end, it's not even about that. This would be too much, but because I think conceptually, some people would understand that in the end, it's just about there being someone or not, but in the end, what comes from this message, so to speak, it's not even that. It's not making up that duality. I think that's the problem basically for the person, why it can't get it at all. Because I know some people for whom it seems to be the most important thing to get rid of this illusion of "I," as if nothing (else in the world) matters, but this doesn't matter.

Justin Allen: Yeah. But even that, that way that you're describing a person that wants to get rid of the "I," let's say, they want to be "there" to get rid of the "I."

Andreas Müller: Absolutely. Oh, totally.

Justin Allen: That's what I mean (excitedly speaking). When you say it, or to me, that's the crazy message to me, is that it's really not like... That is such a radical thing in a way, when you think it's really about...

Andreas Müller:	Death.
Justin Allen:	Yeah. I don't like to use the word death (here in this context). I want to try to avoid using the word death because I think it's too loaded (spiritually).
Andreas Müller:	All right. Yeah. That's fine. (laughing)
Justin Allen:	I think that you have to... Not that you have to, but it's like a natural thing to me to want to come up with my own way of saying it or my own word or at least to change it all the time.
Andreas Müller:	Yeah. I think death sounds... I think for me, death is... It's beautifully unspiritual. I mean more correct would be to say "no self," for example, that's what the person is afraid of. Or can't get, "no self," which is not even an action, so to speak, but no self for me sounds kind of spiritual again.
Justin Allen:	Death sounds spiritual to me also.
Andreas Müller:	Yeah. But it's not really what you want. I mean, you can turn it into the spiritual death and the death of the ego, but when you start thinking about what death actually would mean for you, then it's not something you really want, but you're right, of course. I mean, you can turn everything into a high goal, of course.
Justin Allen:	But talking about it as a death or however, "no self" or "no me," the way that I'm going to talk about it right now is "no experience."
Andreas Müller:	Yes, (laughing) which seen from the person would basically be death.
Justin Allen:	Yeah. But it's a different (laughing) way right now...
Andreas Müller:	It sounds more neutral.

Justin Allen:	... death and no experience mean the same thing.
Andreas Müller:	Oh yeah, absolutely.
Justin Allen:	Yeah. And I prefer the neutral way to say it, because death still sounds way too romantic or dramatic...
Andreas Müller:	I also like deep sleep without waking up. (laughing)
Justin Allen:	That's what people wish. That's why you take too many sleeping pills.
Andreas Müller:	Yeah. Well, they just do it because they are quite certain that they're going to wake up again from it, because hardly anyone takes an overdose.
Justin Allen:	Yeah.
Andreas Müller:	It's still not too much (laughing). It's still possible to wake up from it. Then you can take as many pills as you want. Same with beer or drugs.
Justin Allen:	But no experience is... I mean, that concept, if you really remove, not that you can, but if you were to really remove yourself from that, then it's really radical. If you don't move yourself from it, so you're still thinking, "Yeah, I want to have no experience," when you're saying it that way, I want to be the person that has the "no experience - experience" or I want to be the person that loses themselves or... Then it's not radical really because you're just... It could seem radical if that happened to you somehow or you had a moment of "no self" or you thought that you convinced yourself that you weren't there. But the radical thing is really no experience and it's so radical because you can't imagine that situation, by definition, you can't imagine a no-experience situation.
Andreas Müller:	Oh yeah. Of course. I mean, it's radical because it contradicts the person's experience to 100%.

Justin Allen: Yeah, from 100% to 0%.

Andreas Müller: That's the thing, it's the complete opposite to one's own impression. And as you say, everything else would be somehow comprehensible, conceptually digestible, somehow objectified. In a way, no matter how extreme that is, the person can, to some degree, go with it because it would all be within its own realm, so to speak, within the realm of experiencing. But to not be there is the most radical thing for the person because it seems to be like, the greatest opposite to its presence.

Justin Allen: Yeah. But it's not.

Andreas Müller: Well, in the end, not, because its presence isn't real.

Justin Allen: That's the thing, every single thing you say, in a sense, then has to be qualified. And that's where I also see the opportunity for, added confusion, is that it's like how you began. You say, "If there's 'no one' there experiencing." Then they're also by the fact of there not being anything there, you can't really then say, "Yeah, but there are objects, like the rock really does exist." It's just that the sense of you or the identity that you have or whatever, that's the only thing that doesn't exist, but all this other stuff exists (not really, because no one knows). So that's a radical sentence in itself, but it's totally organic and natural from the fact that if there's not somebody there, then of course, it's so obvious of course, then none of this other stuff can exist because there's not anything there to point to it anymore.

Andreas Müller: Absolutely. And not coming from logic, it's not coming from thinking it through and then it turns out that, ah, it must be like that. No, there's just that which made that claim that there is reality, that there is time or space or suffering or seeking or insights. There's just nothing there, which makes that claim anymore. And that's absolutely natural and effortless and ordinary.

Justin Allen:

So all these other kind of... I don't know how to call them, but these branches or these subcategories of your message, or all these other things that come up, they're also... Like when you say... when the death of the "me" happens or when there's no experience anymore, it's not a big deal. Or it's like life goes on the same way. And it's because there isn't a change. There is nothing that actually happened. And also because there's "no one" there either, there can't be any kind of, excitement about it or realization or joy or epiphany, or "I get it" (laughing). Or you can't really say life is better now than it used to be. None of this can happen anymore. And that all comes out in these talks in various ways. And then there's always a lot of questions about, of course, what it's like for you before and after and what changes for you. There are questions like, "Do you go to the grocery store"?

Andreas Müller:

Now, I just go to the boot store (laughing). Yeah, I know what you mean...

Justin Allen:

And hidden in a way, behind all of those (statements or claims) … and you generally are able to bring it back always to, "Oh, there's 'no one' there." But it always escapes (the audience). It always escapes understanding (even superficial or logical understanding). It always escapes understanding because what you're pointing to is the absence of understanding and what you're pointing to is the absence of "getting it" or what you're pointing to is the absence of figuring something out.

Andreas Müller:

Well, in the end, as you say, the absence of the experience in the end, and the rest again just follows, so to speak. So the other things are rather just chatter, just chatting about something.

Justin Allen: The other things are just chatter, yeah.

Andreas Müller: It's rather just chatting. "Are there objects"? or, "No, there aren't objects." "Is there time now"? or, "No, there is not." "Well, why not"? In the end, there's just "no one" there and this blows the whole reality.

Justin Allen: I wanted to also talk about...

Andreas Müller: But chatting isn't wrong, it's whole and complete.

Justin Allen: Yeah. That you say all the time. (laughing)

Andreas Müller: Person might say, but no, it's wonderful.

Justin Allen: Yeah. The other thing that I wanted to talk about was one of the chapters in the book that we did (referring to *No-Point Perspective*) was something about Romeo. Maybe it was just called Romeo or...

Andreas Müller: Yeah. I know.

Justin Allen: Somehow Romeo was in the chapter and somehow the focus in that chapter or the discovery, in a sense, was talking about the character Romeo, from Romeo and Juliet. And how, if I or you were the actor playing Romeo, we would go through all the emotions and storyline of what happened to Romeo. And maybe we'd carry a sword and be in a sword fight at some point and we would lose Juliet, or the threat of losing Juliet would happen to us. So we'd be sad and blah, blah, blah. And it would be totally accepted that after you come off stage that you would no longer be Romeo, that you'd just be Andreas.

Andreas Müller:	Yeah, and it would actually be clear that there never was Romeo.
Justin Allen:	Exactly. The key sentence in a way, it was, "Romeo never existed and..."
Andreas Müller:	Never existed, no matter how it looked, no matter how it felt, no matter how it seemed, Romeo never existed for a single moment.
Justin Allen:	Right. And anytime we see a movie, every single character that's ever been played by any actor or actress, none of those characters, except for the ones where you're maybe pretending to be a person that actually existed, but either way, they never were there.
Andreas Müller:	Yes.
Justin Allen:	As convincing as it is that Romeo is a character... And everybody's read it probably or seen it in their lives, and there's been thousands of plays, Romeo still has never existed.
Andreas Müller:	Yes.
Justin Allen:	And then when you apply that to your life, you never have existed either. (laughing)
Andreas Müller:	Yeah. I keep saying that. Absolutely.
Justin Allen:	And as convincing as it is that you are there, it's just... I'm saying convincing as it is for us (an audience).
Andreas Müller:	Just for the seeker, because that's an important thing.
Justin Allen:	Yeah. So just as it's convincing and it was to you, let's say, like in your storyline, in the past, it was convincing to you that you were there.

Andreas Müller:	Yeah.
Justin Allen:	And then it was obvious, for lack of a better word, it's obvious ("now") that you were never there.
Andreas Müller:	Yeah.
Justin Allen:	And that's a shocking, radical message also.
Andreas Müller:	Only to "someone."
Justin Allen:	Yeah. That's what I'm speaking about though. (laughing)
Andreas Müller:	Yeah. Oh yeah. All right (laughing). Sorry. Yeah, because the death of "I am," so to speak, isn't really radical. It just seems radical for "someone."
Justin Allen:	Right. But that's why I'm trying to use this analogy in a way. It's also not radical for you when you're playing Romeo to come off the stage and not be Romeo anymore.
Andreas Müller:	Yes.
Justin Allen:	Not that you can compare these things, but...
Andreas Müller:	Exactly, that's a difficult thing, you can't really compare them.
Justin Allen:	And the book (*No-Point Perspective*), when we were attempting to compare it, that's how the sentence came out, Romeo never existed.
Andreas Müller:	Exactly. That was the lovely thing about it. That in this whole play, Romeo was never there. But the problem is that, of course, if you have this personalized setup, you still have this person in there playing Romeo. And then also afterwards, knowing that there never was Romeo in the end,

because I know who I really am and that is a personalized picture.

Justin Allen: Right. That's the dilemma of that analogy, is that, when Andreas Müller plays Romeo and then he's done with Romeo, he's still, unfortunately, Andreas. (laughing)

Andreas Müller: Yeah. I noticed that, whenever I finished playing, I just ended up being me again. (laughing)

Justin Allen: That's the same with spirituality, religion, philosophy, therapy, career, family, whatever search you do, whatever your search engine is, and whatever role you play or whatever you think has happened to you, you're still there experiencing it.

Andreas Müller: Yeah, exactly. Yeah. And I was just saying, well, this is important when I said... Well, not really (important), but when I said it would be only like that for the seeker, because you have many spiritual teachings and they use exactly the same analogy. But they are working on "you" getting unconvinced, so to speak, from being "someone," by noticing who you really are, for example. That's why I said, because in many teachings, as I said, they use exactly this example and think that you can somehow find out that you are not real.

Justin Allen: Yeah. Or it's not even that complicated. They're just saying, "You're not really Romeo." They're still saying you are... (awareness)

Andreas Müller: I never was (meaning, Andreas never was Romeo or Andreas).

Justin Allen: You're you, thinking that you're Romeo. And what this is saying is, there never was a Romeo and there's not anything afterwards either. They're saying that Romeo never existed. And in this case of the analogy, there's no going back to Andreas Müller or the...

Andreas Müller: Either. Absolutely.

Justin Allen: ... the original actor.

Andreas Müller: Yeah. To another experience. There is no coming, but... And I get it. Yes. There was no Romeo in the first place, but there also was no, let's say awakening or going back to who I really am as an experienced reality. Yeah, totally. Of course. Absolutely.

Justin Allen: And then if you put that sentence, there never was a Romeo, for you, there never was an Andreas Müller, and that gets said in this message repeatedly too, in a way about how, when Andreas Müller, the experience, was no longer, it's also that it never was, that that never happened and that never existed in the first place.

Andreas Müller: Absolutely. Totally.

Justin Allen: And then that's, to me, the shocking part of this message in a way, is that, what you're really pointing at is "no experience" or from a spiritual perspective, the shocking thing about the message is that there's no awareness or there's not this ultimate, "I'm aware of... I'm just awareness," "of course, I'm not me (epiphany)." I'm awareness that's aware of me. From the spiritual perspective only, that is the shocker, but let's just say from a layman perspective, and I mean layman by somebody that hasn't really been involved in spirituality, religion, or philosophy, they could relate to the message in a way of being shocked kind of, or of interpreting it as radical, when you say that there's that experience or that you think is they're experiencing a self or awareness is actually not happening. It's not there ever, blah, blah.

Justin Allen:	And then the second thing is in the Romeo case or in your case, when you say that also there never was an Andreas Müller, that's a shocking part of the message, I think. In one point you are saying...
Andreas Müller:	Yeah.
Justin Allen:	... But it's shocking to then, in the death, let's say. I know that you don't realize this, but to put it this way, it's shocking to die, and then it's shocking that you never lived.
Andreas Müller:	Yeah (laughing). Not only shocking to die but yes, it could be as shocking to have never really lived (laughing). Yes.
Justin Allen:	And those are the two points of this message in a way, that there never was an experience (or experiencer). There isn't actually experience and there never was experience, even though it seemed like there was experience.
Andreas Müller:	That's the thing. And it actually only seems to be shocking within the person's concepts and beliefs and rounds. Because in the end, it's not shocking at all, but in order to be shocked, so to speak, by these statements or by these apparent statements, you already have to have been in the personal world, because in the end they are not shocking at all, but...
Justin Allen:	Well, they also aren't shocking to a five-year-old because a five-year-old would never necessarily grasp the thing that's being pointed to. So you also have to throw into it, it's shocking because somebody, somehow some part of them understands what's being threatened.
Andreas Müller:	Yeah. One could say so. Yeah.

Justin Allen:	You could go out to talk to a million people and out of the million people, maybe only 1000, maybe they have a sick feeling or they have an excited feeling or whatever, because let's say they get what's being pointed to, maybe 10,000 people feel a certain way because they're understanding it in a different way (that they are not there as an identity, but as awareness). And the majority of them probably it would go in one ear and out the other without any kind of...
Andreas Müller:	Well, or they would dismiss it.
Justin Allen:	Or they wouldn't even dismiss it. It just wouldn't even penetrate them in any way to make a decision of if they dismiss it or not. It would just be indifferently ignored.
Andreas Müller:	No, no, just not a conscious dismissal. They just wouldn't...
Justin Allen:	A nothing - no reaction might happen. It'd be like the falling of a leaf going unnoticed.
Andreas Müller:	Yeah. Oh totally.
Justin Allen:	So that's what I think. I do think this is going to be a bullshit sentence too, but when you really feel or sense, that what's being talked about or pointed to, is that sense of "thereness" or of being there or of the undeniable (sense that I am there), what generally we would consider an undeniable experience. And I think experience is a good word in the sense that it's not... You're not tied into the spirituality of awareness, and it's a common word because everybody's using it... In general, we're trying to gain experiences.
Andreas Müller:	It was a nice experience.

Justin Allen:	Anything's... Even if the worst thing happens to you, you still say, "Well, it was a bad experience, but I learned from it."
Andreas Müller:	Exactly. Oh yeah, yeah.
Justin Allen:	And generally, everybody's definition of what they are is different. Like somebody will say, "I'm just pure awareness." Somebody will say, "I'm a constellation of feelings, emotions, body, mind, whatever." But for every one of those situations, they're only happening because there's an apparent experience that they're there. And that's what's being threatened in a way, or it's not even being threatened because there's no intention, but what's being pointed at is that that experience or that sensed experience is the illusion. And then you would say, "That's not an illusion because it's not happening in the first place anyways."
Andreas Müller:	Yes, exactly.
Justin Allen:	And that's something that's... When I hear it, I just think it's so dumb (laughing). It's such a nothing sentence, you know?
Andreas Müller:	Yes. Absolutely. It's absurd, this whole meeting is absurd.
Justin Allen:	Yeah. And all the sentences are absurd also.
Andreas Müller:	Yes. Oh totally. Right from the start, the whole apparent existence, so to speak, is absurd.
Justin Allen:	But it's also only absurd to "someone."
Andreas Müller:	Again, for the word absurd to make sense, so to speak, it would already need someone living in beliefs and assumptions and someone who thought it would or might make sense. Someone

who thought that this whole reality, including this meeting (laughing) might make sense. It's not absurd, just in contrast to the assumption that it follows rules, is real, makes sense. This is quite absurd, but then you are already again, operating within conceptual reality.

Justin Allen: And then that's when you say you're already operating in... What'd you say, conventional?

Andreas Müller: Conceptual.

Justin Allen: When you're operating on a conceptual basis, that's already pointing to the illusion of somebody there and that concept, the conceiving that's going on, and the conditioning and the collection of concepts are the tangle or the web that generally people that are listening to this message are trying to unravel. Or they think that by listening to this message potentially that web of concepts might get unraveled.

Andreas Müller: Yes. Maybe it even would.

Justin Allen: Yeah. Maybe it even would, but it wouldn't be because of this message or because of anything.

Andreas Müller: Yeah. It would just be what apparently happens. Yeah, absolutely.

Justin Allen: And that sentence, that would be what apparently happens and having to qualify everything you say with the precursor of apparently is just because of, the first fundamental illusion of being there in the first place.

Andreas Müller: Yeah, absolutely.

Justin Allen: So that to me, is something that I want to point out in a way, is that, just because of that fundamental illusion and this whole feeling, the whole feeling of there being a web of things or layers, like the Buddhist, I don't know if it's a Buddhist saying, but the peeling of the onion, some spirituality says something about the peeling away of the onion layers (laughing). And that's what it seems like you have to do, it's because if there's this center or this core that you're trying to get at, then of course you have to dissect or deconstruct or somehow...

Andreas Müller: Separate the unreal from the real, so to speak.

Justin Allen: Yeah. And that's why it always seems like with this, that there's some work involved. And then when people listen to your message, they superficially get excited, "Ah, look, I don't have to do anything," because that's a commonly misinterpreted idea, is that nobody has to do anything to get to where they wish that they could get, to understand the message.

Andreas Müller: That's the thing. The person might hear, "Oh great, I don't have to do anything in order to become enlightened."

Justin Allen: Right, which is true. (laughing)

Andreas Müller: No, it's not true because no one will ever become enlightened. (laughing)

Justin Allen: Yeah. But that's what's true. You don't...(laughing)

Andreas Müller: That's the problem with that stand.

Justin Allen: You don't have to do anything to get enlightened is true. I mean, you try to say it, you try to correct it and say, "There's nothing you can do to..."

Andreas Müller: Exactly. But that's what the person would be very joyful about. They would only hear, "Oh great,

I don't need to do anything," but it would still somehow end up having this idea that it'll become fulfilled at some point in the future. Just the good news is that I don't have to do anything for it.

Justin Allen: Right. It's like the unemployment check.

Andreas Müller: Yeah, exactly.

Justin Allen: So then, like you say all the time, there's... To that message, I think you say, somebody will say, "So I don't have to do anything?" And then you'll correct it and say, "No, it's not that you don't have to do anything, it's that you're not there."

Andreas Müller: Yeah. There isn't anyone...

Justin Allen: ...somebody there to do something.

Andreas Müller: Yeah.

Justin Allen: And that's the radical thing, that's the pointing at the radical thing to that person. But that person then can't, just by the nature of the illusory experience of being a person, they can't grasp that message. And if they did grasp it, then...

Andreas Müller: Well, I'm not even really speaking to anyone. I'm not talking to them. In a way, it's more like, "Well, I'm just saying."

Justin Allen: Yeah, words are just coming from where you are. But I'm saying that when somebody hears that, first, there's the misconception that you're saying, "Don't do anything," which you're not saying. And then you point out, "I'm not saying that you don't do anything. What I'm saying is that you're not there." And that's what then gets kind of... It goes over the head, and I'm saying it goes over the head because naturally, if there's somebody there on the other side of this message, then it has to go over their head because... (there is no head to go over)

Andreas Müller: Absolutely.

Justin Allen: I think going over the head is a good analogy in a sense, because you're not capable of addressing someone. (laughing)

Andreas Müller: It's impossible. Oh absolutely. There's just not anyone there. Yeah. Automatically, the same thing. It's automatic.

Justin Allen: Automatically and naturally for you, there can't be an addressing of somebody's question or somebody's problem, or if they get it or not get it.

Andreas Müller: Impossible. Yeah. There isn't anyone.

Justin Allen: And so, by definition, this message, I'm just trying to get to some of the things that come out in these talks all the time. By definition, that's why these talks have no meaning and they're not going to give you anything. They're not going to do anything because there's not somebody there for it to do anything too, or this message can't modify somebody. It can't affect somebody.

Andreas Müller: Yeah. Totally.

Justin Allen: And it can't affect anybody because there just isn't anybody.

Andreas Müller: Yes. It's automatic.

Justin Allen: Yeah. And then it's also automatic for you in the case of you being the you as "no experiencer." I mean, you can't be that, but the no experiencing Andreas Müller (laughing) by nature...

Andreas Müller:	"Hi Andreas. That's Andreas." "Who is it"? "He's the guy who doesn't experience." "Ah, all right." Sorry. (laughing)
Justin Allen:	But that's why you say, somebody might say, "Why do you do this"? And then you have to say, "Well…" Ultimately you have to say, "I don't know why I do this. I'm not really here doing this." You can't really provide an answer for that.
Andreas Müller:	No. There is no answer.
Justin Allen:	And that's why you also say there's no answer. I can't answer your questions. Or maybe you say, "I don't know, this is just a reaction, I guess, kind of."
Andreas Müller:	I don't know. It's just what seems to be happening. Man, if I would say I don't know, the other person might say, "Well, then you have to dig deeper." (laughing)
Justin Allen:	Yeah. They think you are dodging the question.
Andreas Müller:	Yeah.
Justin Allen:	I would say that's it. That's it for me.
Andreas Müller:	All right. Cool. I see that some people are raising their hand already.

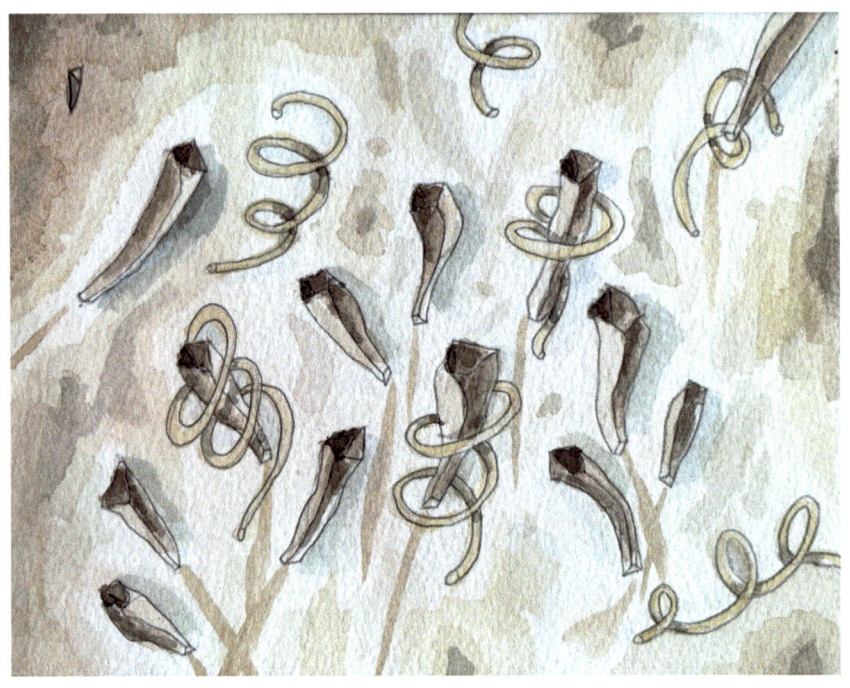

I ROBOT

Andreas Müller:	Do you have anything to say at all actually? (laughing)
Justin Allen:	Yeah, that I do.
Andreas Müller:	All right.
Justin Allen:	So, I actually read through parts of our book again (*No-Point Perspective*).
Andreas Müller:	Yeah.
Justin Allen:	And while I was reading, I jotted down some, not passages from the book, but some paraphrasing that I wanted to reread to you and have your feedback.
Andreas Müller:	All right.
Justin Allen:	And there's a little bit of a structure, so I'm just going to start chronologically with the way that they came to me, these notes. And then maybe there's a structure where then we go back and revIsIt It or that it unravels. So I wrote this one passage that I'm going to read to you, and then immediately after though, I want to read it another way.
Andreas Müller:	Okay. (laughing)

Justin Allen:	This first note says, "The dilemma is that there is no dilemma, and if there is an apparent dilemma, it might mean there is a point with a question like, what's the point?" And so I reread that today before we started talking and then I wanted to reword it. (laughing)
Andreas Müller:	Okay.
Justin Allen:	So I say, "If there is or would be a dilemma, it would be an apparent dilemma. And if there is an apparent dilemma, it suggests a position, an apparent position, or an apparent point, which might ask the question, what's the point? And only an apparent point would or could have this question."
Andreas Müller:	Yes. Just yes (laughing). That's exactly what I meant.
Justin Allen:	Do you see the subtle difference between the two? (laughing)
Andreas Müller:	No, actually, no.
Justin Allen:	Okay.
Andreas Müller:	The last one was more clear and better English.
Justin Allen:	Maybe. Well, the first one assumes a couple things and the second one was a little bit more qualitative; I think.
Andreas Müller:	Like a statement.
Justin Allen:	Yeah.
Andreas Müller:	Yeah. All right.
Justin Allen:	So then from that let's say it expands a little, and then I wrote, "Questions like who am I could arise

where you are, meaning you Andreas over there. Questions like, "who am I"? could arise where you are, but because there is 'no one' there, that question could never really develop. But if that question were to arise where there is a supposed someone, it could spark a dilemma, but the question would not be the dilemma, instead it would be the supposed point supposedly questioning and/or knowing that question."

Andreas Müller: All right. I didn't really get the last part, to be honest. And I know what you mean, but I would say when there is "no one," it's not really that the question could arise.

Justin Allen: Right. And that goes back to that first note where I said, that question couldn't arise for you.

Andreas Müller: Yeah, exactly. It just doesn't arise. Yeah.

Justin Allen: So what I say though, is that, if that question were to arise for someone, and let's say - now it could only arise for a supposed someone.

Andreas Müller: So to speak, they go together, the person and that question can't be separated really.

Justin Allen: Yeah.

Andreas Müller: Yes.

Justin Allen: Okay. But then that's a little bit different. So let me put it this way. If the supposed someone has a question arise like, "What am I"? or, "Who am I"? or, "What's the meaning of this"? They would assume that the question is the problem or they would assume the question is the dilemma. You know what I mean?

Andreas Müller: Yeah, I think they would actually assume that not having the answer is the dilemma.

Justin Allen: Okay. But the question presents a dilemma, let's
                  say.

Andreas Müller: Yeah.

Justin Allen: They don't suppose that the dilemma is, first of all,
                  that there's this position that even could have this.

Andreas Müller: Yes, exactly.

Justin Allen: So that's what that's saying. It just says, if that
                  question were to arise where there is a supposed
                  someone, it could spark a dilemma, but the
                  question would not be the dilemma, instead it
                  would be the supposed point.

Andreas Müller: Yes, absolutely. Yeah. Then they go together in the
                  end.

Justin Allen: Yeah. That's something that I didn't write then.

Andreas Müller: Yeah.

Justin Allen: So those are the first two notes.

Andreas Müller: Okay.

Justin Allen: The third one I have, "It is in fact only existential
                  questions that seem to be problems because by
                  definition they assume existence."

Andreas Müller: Yes.

Justin Allen: So that would just be a take on these existential
                  dilemmas and then these existential questions are
                  just really because existence is, first of all, assumed
                  and because, in a sense, because of that initial
                  assumed position of existence, then an unraveling
                  of potential other seeming dilemmas come from
                  that initial first position.

Andreas Müller:	Yes.
Justin Allen:	So I wrote down as notes (laughing) as two types of questions, one that would arise for you might be, "What should I eat (laughing)?", let's say, which isn't an existential problem. (laughing)
Andreas Müller:	Well yeah, the person could even turn this into an existential problem, but I know what you mean. Absolutely. Yes.
Justin Allen:	But a question that wouldn't arise for you is, "What am I"? or "Who am I"?
Andreas Müller:	Yes. Or which meal will make me happy… (fulfilled)
Justin Allen:	Yeah.
Andreas Müller:	Yeah.
Justin Allen:	And then that's what I wanted to question is those two different types of questions. Let's just say one question is an existential question and another question is just questioning, like just a …
Andreas Müller:	Mm-hmm (affirmative).
Justin Allen:	Neither one. It's not that both of them, in your case, both questions don't assume existence, but in a case where there is someone there's a clear distinction. Both questions assume an existence.
Andreas Müller:	That's the thing. Yeah. Seen from a person both do.
Justin Allen:	And then generally you could say one causes a problem and the other doesn't necessarily. Let's say in the typical "me" or the typical someone, that generally what you're supposed to eat isn't an existential dilemma, generally speaking, but "Who

am I"?, or "What am I"?, or "What's my meaning"?, or "What's my purpose in life"? Those are dilemma questions.

Andreas Müller: Yeah. But actually only because of the difference of the meaning, because in the end for the question of what do I eat, may play the exact same role in the person's idea of fulfillment than the question who am I. So it's not really that the one question totally matters seen from the person and the other question doesn't matter at all. It's actually just the difference in the importance. But I think that there may be people who are much more interested in what they eat and depend on much more joy and luck from that, and they are totally not interested in who they are (laughing), for example.

Justin Allen: Right, good point. But I just meant, what you're saying is totally true, but I meant it more, the food one might be a bad example, but let's just say that...

Andreas Müller: Yeah, I know...

Justin Allen: ... always one (one of the questions) is an existential "problem," there's always questions or potential existential problems, and then there are questions that are just...

Andreas Müller: More functional stuff.

Justin Allen: Exactly.

Andreas Müller: When does the train leave? Stuff like that. Yeah.

Justin Allen: And in the case of "no one" being there, then every question is just, let's say, a functioning question.

Andreas Müller: Absolutely. Oh, yes. Only in that sense, there's only functioning and functional stuff. Yeah.

Justin Allen:	And only those type of questions would apparently arise.
Andreas Müller:	Yes. It's a human functioning, it's not as robotic as it sounds, but in the end, yes. Yeah. It's just functioning.
Justin Allen:	So, then all that suggests ... is that assumed ... that very first assumed position. And then from that assumed position, then it branches out to however it branches out. And the ways that it branches out are how you seek meaning through A, B, C, D, or E.
Andreas Müller:	Yeah.
Justin Allen:	Or whatever it might be.
Andreas Müller:	Yeah. That's why it's basically that if there would be a question, this would be the only question, if is there someone, the rest is actually just detail, it doesn't really matter. Because when you're someone you get the whole dream, and when there isn't someone, the whole dream just pops (explodes, collapses, disappears, etc.).
Justin Allen:	And then two points that come from that are, for example, the question who am I is automatically from someone.
Andreas Müller:	Yeah. In that sense, when there is a real interest, when there is a real question, who am I?
Justin Allen:	A genuine what am I?
Andreas Müller:	Exactly, yes.
Justin Allen:	That already is the illusory experience of a self or of a position.

Andreas Müller: Yeah. Yes. That is the person.

Justin Allen: And what happens in general, what happens is as soon as that illusory position presents itself or is there, it's already missed in a sense.

Andreas Müller: So to speak.

Justin Allen: It's already accepted in a sense.

Andreas Müller: Automatically, yes.

Justin Allen: Exactly.

Andreas Müller: Yes.

Justin Allen: So you can't, at that point … there's not a possibility of even acknowledging that "point" in the sense of it's something there that happened. It's already just that's the foundation, or that's it in every way that it manifests itself.

Andreas Müller: Yes, totally. Yeah. Or everything apparently of course. But yes.

Justin Allen: And so then the second point of that is, let's say the fact is that position isn't there. (laughing)

Andreas Müller: I like that. The fact is, yeah (laughing). What we truly say is… yes exactly.

Justin Allen: But that sense, which is assumed automatically from, day one, or from the morning when you wake up, it's automatically the basis for not everything, but in general, everything that's happening is happening to this assumed position that's already, ignored because it's so fundamental.

Andreas Müller: Yes. Seen from the person, but it's only seen from the person like that. But of course, my presence is the basis for all that I'm aware of, for all that I experience.

Justin Allen: Right.

Andreas Müller: So that's the basis of my life, which is basically everything, all that the person knows is just "me" and my life. Yes.

Justin Allen: And so then to go back to the second part of it, I don't want to even use the word think, I'd say sense, or take for granted, or something.

Andreas Müller: Yeah. That's the weird thing. For the person this just is its world, felt, sensed, thought, it's a holistic experience, but seen from the person, that is the only experience.

Justin Allen: Right. But there actually isn't experience.

Andreas Müller: Exactly. It doesn't have any substance at all. It never happens. While it happens, it's never something, it does not exist, so to speak.

Justin Allen: And that was something that I thought was interesting from our book (*No-Point Perspective*) also, is that we came to that point of, you call the "me" the me, or a someone, or person, or the ego, or awareness, or whatever all the words are for it. But then I thought it was interesting to use the word experience to re-name it ... In a way that seemed a creative way to, describe that, is to call a person an experience, or "personing" or something is experience. It's another way of reducing the person to just being a "me" or a someone as "experience."

Andreas Müller: Yeah. A set up of experiencing. Yeah.

Justin Allen: It's another thing that you can't fathom, or grasp, or understand is how life would be if you can't experience.

Andreas Müller:	Absolutely. (laughing)
Justin Allen:	If it was true as a fact, again, that there's no such thing as experience, then it's another dead end, it's another place where you can't go anywhere.
Andreas Müller:	Yes, absolutely.
Justin Allen:	What's it like (laughing) for there to be no experience? (Rhetorical question)
Andreas Müller:	Yes, exactly. In the end that's the only thing that's not even imaginable, is my impression, but it's just not possible to somehow go there from the personal experience, what this would be like, what's this supposed to be.
Justin Allen:	Yeah.
Andreas Müller:	I think at least. (laughing)
Justin Allen:	And another way that we talked about that was to imagine a robot, or in the case of when we were talking (previously from *No-Point Perspective* talks) we imagined it as a computer, and generally we don't attribute consciousness or at least human awareness, let's say, or experience to a computer.
Andreas Müller:	Yeah.
Justin Allen:	So computer, we attribute function, pure functioning.
Andreas Müller:	Yes. (laughing)
Justin Allen:	And you do the reverse. (laughing)
Andreas Müller:	So maybe I am a robot. (laughing)
Justin Allen:	Yeah. But what we did is an experiment, maybe you could call it a thought experiment, if you could

take experience, if it were something that was reproducible (or even actually existed), or you could produce experience and put it into a chip, or into a USB stick, or something, and you could connect it into your computer and then give the computer the ability to experience.

Andreas Müller: Yeah. (laughing)

Justin Allen: So before, the computer, you were using, it was your own personal computer and you were using it, and typing on it, and looking through the internet with it, and it was performing all the tasks that you gave it and that it was programmed to do. But for all those years, you had your computer for five years, for five years it wasn't aware of you typing on the computer, and it wasn't aware of switching from one website to the next. And now all of a sudden because you gave it this quality of experience (experience and awareness can be interchangeable), it suddenly becomes aware out of nowhere (laughing). To the computer it would be all of a sudden, it's there experiencing tapping and switching websites. (Like waking up in the morning for a person – all of a sudden it is there)

Andreas Müller: Yeah.

Justin Allen: And as soon as that happened it would think, if we follow the logic of the human (experience), it would start to complain maybe, "Why are you tapping me"?

Andreas Müller: Exactly. "Not so hard. Why are you typing on me"? (laughing)

Justin Allen: Exactly.

Andreas Müller: Yes, it would. It would start to seek or maybe try to escape.

Justin Allen:	And then, because there's a position now, whereas before in the computer there wasn't a position, now that there's a (apparent) position it also is aware that for eight hours out of the day there's no tapping, or there's tapping on it and then there's no tapping, and then it goes to sleep when you close the laptop, and then it wakes up again and then it's there again.
Andreas Müller:	That's a sweet picture (laughing). I'm sorry. Yeah.
Justin Allen:	And so for that computer, it might start to get aggravated that it's there and question itself, its very nature of existence, and go through the whole apparent dilemma that seems to happen to the majority of us (humans). But in this computer example, how could it ever get rid of experience… because you programmed it into it, you externally connected and put it into it (it had nothing to do with experience or getting experience). So how could the computer ever go back to how it was before (rhetorical question)? Unless there was no before because there wasn't a position. There is no before for the computer, because before the fake position that you externally inserted into it there was nothing.
Andreas Müller:	Yep.
Justin Allen:	And then as a something, in this case of the computer, because the computer can't itself remove the experience (the external hard-drive or experience chip) that you put into it, the only way it would happen for the computer is if you removed it again.
Andreas Müller:	Yeah.
Justin Allen:	And if you removed it again, then that computer would not know anything about what had happened while this experience-chip was inserted into it?

Andreas Müller: Yeah.

Justin Allen: And it wouldn't be aware of time, there would be no awareness, it'd be in no position for anything to be happening.

Andreas Müller: Yeah. That's basically how I am now (laughing). Yes.

Justin Allen: You still have memory of before though. (laughing)

Andreas Müller: I never claimed that this is a good place to be. (laughing)

Justin Allen: When I think about things that you've talked about and when people ask you about what it's like for you and everything, then that could be a way of creating a scenario where if there were, let's say for you, there never actually was a "me."

Andreas Müller: Yeah, there is "no me." Yes.

Justin Allen: But there never was.

Andreas Müller: There never was - correct.

Justin Allen: There was never an experience ever in your whole life.

Andreas Müller: Yes.

Justin Allen: In your story you say there's a phase though where it seemed to be that you were experiencing.

Andreas Müller: Yes.

Justin Allen: And so the computer, maybe somebody that's a little bit better with IT and technology and stuff might explain. You could imagine even with the computer scenario that because the computer has its own hardware and stuff like that, that those two years that you had inserted the experience-chip into it, even when you removed it, there still might be a memory as a back-up or data log or something...

Andreas Müller: Some traces maybe found in the data that there must have been something that was self-aware, but without knowing what that actually was.

Justin Allen: Exactly. (laughing) And then if people (other computers) were to talk to you, if there were other computers there that were trying to communicate with you (the other computer), there's three other computers lying around here, and these three other ones had the awareness-chip inserted into them, they would just be other computers around with this fake experiencing happening.

Andreas Müller: Yeah (laughing). And what I'm thinking right now, that shows that this message is really 21st century. We had to wait for the computers to get the perfect description of what this message is about (laughing).

Justin Allen: I was thinking about how I remember when you first told me one of the ... the supposed big shocks of experience dropping away is that there never was experience.

Andreas Müller: Yeah. In that sense, dropping away, that's the problem with all the pictures that it sounds as if there really was something happening and then it wasn't happening anymore.

Justin Allen: Right. But in this conversation, we're saying it never happens, we're starting off with that.

Andreas Müller: Yeah.

Justin Allen:	We're saying that, when there's the blind seeing (laughing) that there's no experiencer and there's no experiencing and there also never was, then to somebody that is experiencing that seems shocking in a way. (or could seem)
Andreas Müller:	Yeah.
Justin Allen:	And then the way that you tell it, you also tell it as if there's two surprises, the one surprise is what you call the death of "me," which I would want to put another way, but let's just say the death of the "me," and then realizing that there never was a "me."
Andreas Müller:	And they go together. That's one thing actually.
Justin Allen:	Yeah. But I'm saying the way that you've talked about it sometimes, at least it's been interpreted by me for sure, I'm saying in the past, and from our talks, and maybe what I've read from you, then it seems like there's the death of the "me" and then there's the clarity or the obviousness that there actually also never was a "me."
Andreas Müller:	Understand, yeah. Understand, yeah. But actually...
Justin Allen:	They go together.
Andreas Müller:	Yeah, it's the same thing actually.
Justin Allen:	Yeah. OK.
Andreas Müller:	Yeah. The moment when it becomes obvious that there is "no me," that's also the death of it, the melting away of it.
Justin Allen:	Yeah.
Andreas Müller:	Which isn't really logical.

Justin Allen: So, that's it then. (laughing)

Andreas Müller: Cool. All right. So anyone (laughing) who wants to comment on that or ask something independently from that, feel free.

*This was the last talk where the audiece could ask follow-up questions and join us in the conversation.

POST-LIFE

Andreas Müller:	All right, it's recording (laughing).
Justin Allen:	So (laughing)... The thing that I was wondering about, it seems like, "I don't know" is an important three words for this message (laughing). Do you agree with me (laughing)?
Andreas Müller:	Yes and no, because even this simple statement (laughing) leaves a huge space for misunderstanding, so to speak.
Justin Allen:	The misunderstanding that you mean, because the one way it can be misinterpreted is that there's still somebody there that doesn't know.
Andreas Müller:	That it's a position. Exactly.
Justin Allen:	But if you take away the position, then it's an important part of this message (laughing).
Andreas Müller:	Absolutely. Then it's the message (laughing).
Justin Allen:	Exactly. Then it's the message. Yeah. Yeah. I wanted to say that there's a big "I don't know" over there for you.
Andreas Müller:	Yes. Yeah.
Justin Allen:	It made me wonder, in the difficulty of talking about this message, I was imagining, in a way it's

like... If you say it's a big, "I don't know" and then you try to say, "Well, what does that mean or how do I understand that"? In some sense, it's just a sense of not knowing anything and not having a position at all. Not that it's a sense, not that it can be anything, but...

Andreas Müller: Yeah.

Justin Allen: It was just intriguing to me because "I don't know" is one of my favorite sayings. I say it, of course or I've said it, of course, as a position, but maybe also not...

Andreas Müller: (laughing) But it's also a comfortable position.

Justin Allen: Not for anybody else. (laughing)

Andreas Müller: That's true (laughing). That's true.

Justin Allen: If anybody asks you, they want you to know.

Andreas Müller: I know.

Justin Allen: If somebody asks you a question, they want there to be some (relatively clear) answer in the... (laughing)

Andreas Müller: Yeah. I have this at home a lot (laughing).

Justin Allen: Yeah, exactly (laughing). I've had it my whole life also. When I've said it... In the beginning, when I would say it, I felt uncomfortable saying I don't know sometimes.

Andreas Müller: It's not very convenient.

Justin Allen: But superficially, you're saying, "do you want to go here or here? I don't know." That's kind of a position. Do you want to go left or do you want to go right? You say, "I don't know." Then in that sense, it's just a position in this circumstance of a decision to make.

Andreas Müller: Yeah. Yeah. Exactly. For the person, it would be a way to deal with that question, so to speak.

Justin Allen: But then I can't deny in a sense that there's also a reality of just really not knowing and not knowing because you're also not there. If you weren't there, you really wouldn't know anything. There would just always be, "I don't know" for every single situation.

Andreas Müller: Absolutely. Yes. Yeah.

Justin Allen: That's what I mean, in this context of this discussion that we're having. That's the big "I don't know." That's what I'm calling the big "I don't know." It's there as a cloud in a sense, that it's a cloud that's encompassing everything.

Andreas Müller: Yeah. Yes.

Justin Allen: So when you have that, as a person, nobody knows either. Right? But sometimes all the people that think that they're people. They also equally don't know as much as you don't (laughing) know.

Andreas Müller: Yes, absolutely (laughing). Yes.

Justin Allen: Even when they're convinced that they know, they don't know. From your non-position or from this message, that's just an "I don't know," happening as "I know" that the world is made up of matter or I know that the world is made up of spirits or money rules everything. I know that it's still "I don't know," happening as an "I know."

Andreas Müller: Yes. I would say the apparent knowing of the world is made out of meta (beyond), is the unknown. Yeah. It's equally unknown as everything else.

Justin Allen: Yeah. Then the only difference, which is what you will have to always say is an apparent difference between you who outwardly says "I don't know" and then me as a physicist that says, "well, I don't know much, but I know that..."

Andreas Müller: I know (laughing). I don't know much, but I know who I am. I know my name. I know my whole family. I know there's a world. I know that there's a universe (laughing). I know what a table is, what a room is, what air is, what the window is, what cars are. I don't know much, but...

Justin Allen: But I know this (laughing). What's happening to that apparent person when they think that they know is just that it's basically, they think that they are something that's a position that can then confirm these things that they know or not know. That is just a happening. That's not really happening or it's just a happening that's happening as much as anything else that seems to be happening, like cloud, car, wall, hand, whatever.

Andreas Müller: Yeah.

Justin Allen: So when I say as a physicist, or I say as a priest, or I say as a broker on Wall Street, whatever, that I know something, all that's happening is... From this message, would just be an illusion is happening (a story is forming from a fundamental illusion of there being someone – a me – a person – an experience).

Andreas Müller: Well, it would be what happens, but it would be unknown.

Justin Allen: Yeah. But I mean, the illusion would be... The difference between you and that wall street broker or you and that scientist or you and that priest would be, that you're admittedly saying, "I don't know and I can't know because there's no one here that could ever claim to know anything. There's no position here that could confirm or deny (anything)." Whereas they would still think that at least there's some position. Even if they don't have it, they would be sure that somebody does or that it's possible to get, let's say.

Andreas Müller: Yeah. Yes. Yes.

Justin Allen: That difference between that person making that claim and then this message would just be, there's a... Well, that's what I'm calling the illusion, but that would be the... If there's a way to make a distinction or a difference, the difference would simply just be that position that they think is happening.

Andreas Müller: Yes. Yes. Absolutely.

Justin Allen: From this message, you're able to, see that that could be happening to people where they think that they're there.

Andreas Müller: Yes.

Justin Allen: Yeah.

Andreas Müller: That's the funny thing that, so to speak, this message doesn't see the difference between those two while from their apparent perspective, there seems to be a difference. Well, because their impression is also wholeness. Not as a conceptual thing. I just do not experience it as separate. I don't say it from a concept like, "This is wholeness too." No, it very directly is what seems to be happening. But from the person's perspective, what I talk about seems to be something else, seems to be not part of one's experience.

Justin Allen: From this message, and from what's happening over there, there's a big "I don't know" or there's just nothing or just, "I don't know," that's not possible for the person to relate to or even identify with. Even that, when you say that, they just think, "Oh, that'd be so great to have a position of I don't know and to be comfortable not knowing."

Andreas Müller: Yes. Exactly. That's what I mean. Even in that example for the person, that's something they don't know what I speak of when I say not knowing, not experiencing. For them, it's something they can't access from their experience. Yeah.

Justin Allen: Playing this game a little bit further, then let's say that you once were one of these people that was convinced that you were there (laughing).

Andreas Müller: That's what seemed to have happened. Yes. Nicely put (laughing).

Justin Allen: That's what (apparently) happened for part of your life, you were convinced for sure that you knew something.

Andreas Müller: Yeah. Believe me, I knew a lot, and I was willing to tell everyone who was partly interested (laughing).

Justin Allen: Yeah. Or got stuck with you in an elevator.

Andreas Müller: Yeah, exactly (laughing). Oh, the poor people around me (laughing), especially parents, I think. Well, yeah.

Justin Allen: So when you are one of those people (laughing), and then all of a sudden there was one day when you knew something and maybe it didn't happen suddenly, it doesn't matter but all of a sudden, now you don't know anything. That's such a weird thing because you don't even know that you don't know anything (laughing).

Andreas Müller: Exactly. Yes. Yes.

Justin Allen:	Yeah. That would be...
Andreas Müller:	But that's what makes it okay again.
Justin Allen:	Yeah, right. But it's such a... Even from your current non-position, in a way, it's such a blurry... It's like a blur basically because you can't... "blur," do you know the word?
Andreas Müller:	Yeah. Well...
Justin Allen:	I'm using the word blur in the sense that it's like you're in such a deep gray zone in the sense of... let's say that there's black and white and it's very clear that there's black and white and then it's clear, okay, there's middle area (gray) too, but you can still see black and you can still see white. You're in such a blur that there can't even be black and white and there can't even be gray. It's just so blurry that there's nothing. (I do not mean that it is blurry in the sense that it is not clear – I was trying to infer that there is just no position, but apparently things happen anyways – a no-knowing non-position)
Andreas Müller:	Yeah. Yes.
Justin Allen:	So you can't even say that there's nothing. You can't feel like there's nothing because you can't feel. So it's just a big "I don't know" without a position.
Andreas Müller:	That's the natural reality. That's all there is. Yes.
Justin Allen:	And when you say that, the person here senses you're saying it with confidence but you're not. There's not even confidence.
Andreas Müller:	Yes. Because then I would know that. Yes.
Justin Allen:	That's why you can't talk about this well or I mean,

you actually talk about it well, but it doesn't seem like you can talk about it well. Even from/for you, it doesn't seem like you can talk about it well because...

Andreas Müller: I can't.

Justin Allen: Yeah. You can't talk about it well either, because for you, there's not a position which would make it possible to talk about it well. So even for you, in a sense, would have to... as you're speaking and trying... First of all, you're not trying, but as you're speaking and you're talking about this message, for you the whole time, it's all unclear and unknown. And all these words that are coming out have no meaning, have no place, have no position, have no thing that you can pinpoint.

Andreas Müller: Yes, on the one hand, it's pretty indescribable because It's not coming from a position and from knowledge, but it's also not just "blah, blah, blahing" something out. It's quite direct in a way, but yes, it's not coming from...

Justin Allen: But it's totally unknown still. Even if you said, all of a sudden, let's say that you figured out, it just came to you the best possible sentence to describe this (laughing), it'd still be as meaningless as the worst possible sentence (laughing).

Andreas Müller: Yes, absolutely. Yes. Yeah. Yeah.

Justin Allen: Because the only way that you could add worth, is to have a position and one, to be better than the other, not even that could ever happen.

Andreas Müller: Absolutely. You're totally right.

Justin Allen: In that sense, everything you say is as equally important or as equally unimportant as whatever else you're going to say.

Andreas Müller:	Absolutely.
Justin Allen:	Anything you say, it's a stream basically of unknowingness or "I don't knowness" or...
Andreas Müller:	Absolutely. Totally.
Justin Allen:	Even for you, as you say it and as you hear yourself say it in the past, it's immediately like air. It's immediately vapor and...
Andreas Müller:	It never becomes solid. Not for one second.
Justin Allen:	Yes. So even for you, even if you were, as you were saying the most perfect sentence, let's say that there was some fleeting appreciation but... (laughing)
Andreas Müller:	Sweet (laughing). No. Yeah. I know what you mean, but yeah. Yeah.
Justin Allen:	For you, it has to be... It's such an "I don't know." That's the only thing that you can hang onto (I mean attribute) in a sense is the I don't know. But you can't hang onto it at all, but I've been saying that's the only thing that you could... That's why I started off saying, it's an important three words to the message because you say it in many different ways, like you say, oh, it's not knowing or there's just not knowing. There's nothing that you can know.
Andreas Müller:	Yeah. But it's also dangerous. As I said in the beginning, it's also dangerous. I can tell a story about that if you want me to.
Justin Allen:	The person will attach that as something to seek out and say (or weaponize), "I don't know." Of course, they can use it however they want to argue, oh, I don't know what...

Andreas Müller: Yeah. That's what I tell you in a few minutes. So there's a whole story about that. But actually, the best sentence is actually there is "no one." It's better than "I don't know." I know what you mean with I don't know. It kind of covers it, but in the end, there just is "no one."

Justin Allen: Yeah. That's a good one too but you talk about that one a lot (laughing).

Andreas Müller: Yeah. I know.

Justin Allen: "I don't know" was something I was trying to come at from a different angle (laughing).

Andreas Müller: Yeah, that's fine. May I tell a story?

Justin Allen: Yeah.

Andreas Müller: There is a group of people who actually accuse me with this argument and it got a bit nasty even with those people. It doesn't matter too much, but they exactly say "what is" can't be known and they come to me accusing me, why do you speak for hours and answering questions and providing knowledge? They think I provide knowledge and they think I shouldn't be doing the talks because I don't know. That's exactly where the thin line is. My impression is that there is an understanding on their side that I can't know, but immediately there's a conclusion from that, what that would mean. It's what you said. Here there is no position of "I don't know." There's just not knowing.

Justin Allen: I'm only talking about, maybe in a sense, I mean, it doesn't matter, but I'm just talking about it poetically in a sense of...

Andreas Müller: Yeah. I got that. No problem with that.

Justin Allen:	Because...
Andreas Müller:	Okay. I just wanted to tell you because it's something that's going on in my life right now, seeing some YouTube comments and stuff. It's exactly this huge difference between "I don't know" being not a position and "I don't know" being a position.
Justin Allen:	Well, but it is a dilemma that doesn't matter...
Andreas Müller:	Of course.
Justin Allen:	Like we said, anybody that hears this is going to hear a position inside of whatever it is that you say.
Andreas Müller:	It's not a dilemma for me, to be honest.
Justin Allen:	But a person can, by definition of the way that we're defining a person as an actual thing that's there, means that anything that that hears will turn anything into a position. It always will. For the sake of this discussion, we're pretending that we don't have to worry about that. That's just inevitable and... (laughing)
Andreas Müller:	All right. Good. (Pretends a sigh of relief)
Justin Allen:	I was trying to get at... I was thinking about a kid... how we understand the world (a kid/child) knows less than an adult (Andreas confirms) because we think knowledge in general is acquired and we get more of it as we get older, and then you're a wise person at some point. So a child has less knowledge. The younger that they are, even less knowledge. Then you (as an adult) cherish that. That's what we call innocence, I guess. And enlightenment, the way that you talk about enlightenment, spiritual teachers and whoever, basically, they always say, enlightenment is like back to innocence or child-like wonder. They talk about how everything's new.

So maybe you might hear you or Tony Parsons or a "no one there" person talk about how when the (apparent) "me" drops, then everything becomes new all the time, blah, blah, blah. (Andreas confirms)

Justin Allen: That's what "I don't know" is too. I just wanted to put it back into the context of a person, a normal person when they say, "I don't know" that's kind of like, what's coming out of... Let's say it's a legitimate "I don't know." It's like they got caught off guard and a question came to them or something and they say, "I don't know." Or even that expression "I don't know." That's new, because they don't know. So it's a total openness in a sense even to the person, to say, "I don't know."

Andreas Müller: I wouldn't say so.

Justin Allen: But I'm trying to say so only in the sense that... let's just pretend that as a... Not even pretend. Let's just accept that a person, somebody that's "there" thinks that they're there, goes through life, but there's still moments throughout that person's life when they're not there and there's no recognition of it or acknowledgement of it. As a default when you're in deep sleep, let's say as a default position, deep sleeping, you're not there. Also throughout the day, there's 12 hours that you're at work or reading a book or whatever. There's also moments when literally you're not there. Yeah? So I'm just speaking of it in this way that maybe sometimes when the answer comes to you or there's a moment where you say, "I don't know," and either you say it out loud or it's just happening internally, that I'm wondering, or I'm making the claim a little bit that I don't know sometimes might be a true "I don't know." Even though it immediately turns into a position.

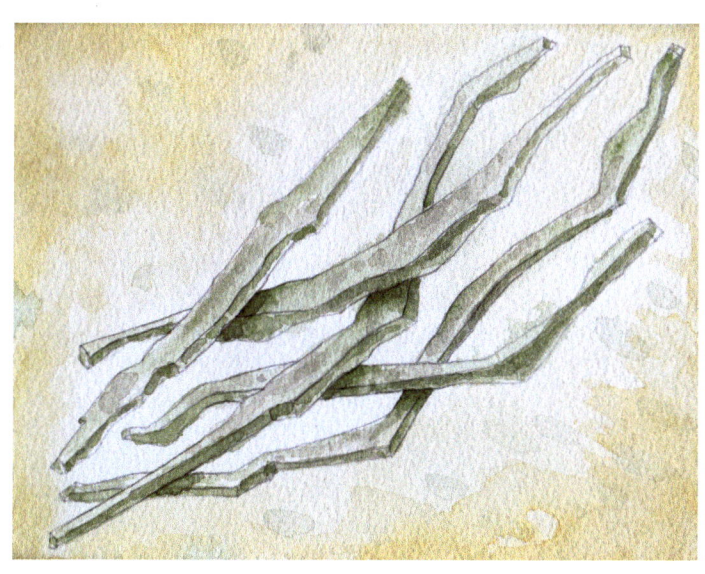

Andreas Müller: I understand. Yeah.

Justin Allen: Let's pretend that there's a... An authentic, "I don't know (laughing)." By an authentic, "I don't know," it means that there's "no one" there that also literally doesn't know. Then immediately it might turn into "I don't know," as a position, but let's say that the origin...

Andreas Müller: Then it's actually a known experience again.

Justin Allen: Exactly. Let's say that the origin before that, was an authentic "I don't know." Then if I look back at my life and I had moments where I said, "I don't know" before it became a position, this is a feeling of I don't know, and is also something that you couldn't talk about (Andreas confirms) because you generally then in that sense, you don't know. So how could you talk about "I don't know" (Andreas confirms)? As you try to talk about, "I don't know," you fall back into the spell, but when the "me" dropped and you were trying to talk about "I don't know," you would never be able to. It would be so impossible to talk about because there's never anything that you could hook into or grab onto. There's never any point.

Andreas Müller: Yeah. But in that sense, you wouldn't even notice it.

Justin Allen: Yeah (excitedly). But that would still be this big cloud in a way. It'd be such a non-happening. Let's say that you were familiar, your whole life with happening, happening and knowing. Now there's not happening and not knowing.

Andreas Müller: Yeah. But it's... Yes?

Justin Allen: What would there be to confirm that or prove it, there'd be nothing?

Andreas Müller:	Exactly.
Justin Allen:	So I don't know what I'm getting at (laughing), but then as a next step, that makes it seem so, I want to say un-wow. What would be impressive about it (laughing)? It would just be, "I don't know." I don't know is such an unsatisfactory thing.
Andreas Müller:	Oh yes. I mean, this whole message is utterly unsatisfactory for the person.
Justin Allen:	Yeah (excitedly). But I even think it's unsatisfactory... I don't think it's unsatisfactory for you but I also think that when it happens, why would there ever be, "oh, my God? Life is so crazy. It's so amazing." I mean, maybe you've talked about what's happening over there to you as it's incredible or it's amazing but at the same time, it's not at all.
Andreas Müller:	Yes. Yeah.
Justin Allen:	To me, one of the best messages or words to come out of your message is the ordinariness or how ordinary it is. To me, even as a person, from a people-person perspective, what's more ordinary than I don't know?
Andreas Müller:	Yeah. One could say so. It's not a very interesting person to talk to (laughing).
Justin Allen:	Yeah (laughing).
Andreas Müller:	Totally (laughing). Of course.
Justin Allen:	The only interesting thing that you can talk about is how you don't know (laughing).
Andreas Müller:	All the varieties of me having no clue at all (laughing). Exactly.

Justin Allen:	How many different ways can you come up with talking about how you don't know anything?
Andreas Müller:	You would need to be a very special person to find this interesting (laughing).
Justin Allen:	Yeah.
Andreas Müller:	It was a compliment actually (laughing).
Justin Allen:	Yeah (laughing), I found my niche (laughing).
Andreas Müller:	(laughing) It won't be of any use, but it will do for a while.
Justin Allen:	Yeah. With 0.001% of the population that also finds nothing interesting or "I don't know" interesting (laughing). So then to put you in the spotlight more, if we just talked for 30 minutes a bit about the three words "I don't know," but mostly let's say from my side, how is "I don't know" from your point of view or from your side (laughing)?
Andreas Müller:	I mean, all that comes to my mind are three words (laughing)... "I don't know." That's the thing, it can't be imagined because it's not even really a cloud. Knowledge. Knowing, or not knowing just isn't something that can be considered at all. That's why it's not even blurry. The idea of blurry... I knew what you meant, but of course the picture of blurry still dances with the idea of clarity, knowing black and white, and then it gets blurry. But there is just nothing to know. This whole complete reality of knowing, as I say, I don't even know what this should be.
Justin Allen:	Yeah. That's what I wanted to talk about though. It's really that you don't know what this should be or what it is or you don't know what's going on.

Andreas Müller: I don't know what's going (laughing)... Yeah. We shouldn't talk about this too loudly. Yeah. It's not only that I don't know what's going on. I don't even know that something is going on. Seen from the person this is so weird. This is so different from what the person's ideas are. It's not really different. As we said in the beginning, it's not really different, but to the person's ideas and beliefs, it's unimaginable in the end. Yeah. That while it is happening, it's completely unknowable.

Justin Allen: Right. Every single future, even though, you can't even say future's happening, there's a future and there's clearly a past, and now there's this moment happening, the moment's turning into the future, and the moment used to be the past, that can't even be confirmed at all.

Andreas Müller: Not at all. Not a single bit.

Justin Allen: Even that confirmation that it can't be confirmed also can't be confirmed (laughing and Andreas confirms). So that's what I was trying to convey with the big "I don't know," I don't know, or the blur, or whatever. That's me trying to talk about it, I guess. But everything that's happening to you isn't even happening. You can't even say there's nothing happening and all that... When you say there's nothing happening, that's just you trying to express this "I don't knowness" or this nothingness that seems to be appearing as whatever.

Andreas Müller: Yes. I mean, the interesting thing is that it's weird to use those words, but it just really is like that. Not really, again, in a sense of knowledge, it's not concepts. I mean, the person might even be able to follow the concepts. Of course, when there's "no one" there, it's logical, nothing can be confirmed or stated, but the personal experience would go on. But the interesting thing is that it just is like that, when this illusion, this felt sense that there is someone who knows when that just collapses. I can't explain that or know that, but it's yeah, honest.

Justin Allen: You know how, in a spiritual sentence of somebody trying to express enlightenment. A typical image might be, I was sitting somewhere and all of a sudden, I was the wall (referring to how enlightened people claim to become one with something - one with the wall, with the trees, with sounds, etc...).

Andreas Müller: The wall?

Justin Allen: The wall. All of a sudden, "I was the wall (I became the wall)." If somebody says that while I'm reading a book from someone "spiritual" and they write, "...I walked around for 10 years and then all of a sudden I was looking at a wall and I became the wall." (laughing)

Andreas Müller: Yes. Felt a bit stiff, but...(laughing).

Justin Allen: If I read that, and start to think, "somebody became a wall?" Maybe a first interpretation is that somebody merged into the wall – became one with an inanimate object. You would never say any sentence like that, would you?

Andreas Müller: Well, maybe I even would, but not really. Yes. Yeah. I know what you mean. Yeah.

Justin Allen: Let's say that you would say that sentence. Let's say that... The way that I would interpret most spiritual books or people that would've said that, they mean that... I think what they would've meant is that they're consciousness and consciousness is everything and they became consciousness and...

Andreas Müller: For example, or that there was an experience of "I'm everything." "I'm the wall" or whatever. Yeah.

Justin Allen:	But if you were to say it, you might have to qualify it in a sense that this is how... At least these are my words, this is me paraphrasing how I think you would say it, you would say that, if you were also the wall, then the only way that could happen from your non-position in a sense would be if there's no position, then how could there be me and wall, there would just be...
Andreas Müller:	Exactly.
Justin Allen:	Yeah.
Andreas Müller:	Yes. There would be... Yeah.
Justin Allen:	That made me think in the very beginning, when you and I started to have the *No-Point Perspective* talks, we started talking about teachers in the first two chapters, and in a sense at the time, I think what I was trying to get at, was how I thought, if we took that sentence that maybe what these spiritual teachers mean when they say, "I became the wall," I was trying to say, maybe that's just their way of saying what you're saying. Back then, that's what we were doing in a way. Then we were saying, "Well, we can't really know what they meant by that, but generally what you're saying and what we said now, is that when a spiritual person or teacher says that, they don't mean that they disappear, and that's why they're saying that they became the wall, what they're saying is, it's more like they merge into this overwhelming thing that seems to be happening where it's all just consciousness, and consciousness is creating the wall, and it's creating the dog, and it's creating everything... You think that you're outside of that consciousness as this ego as a person. Then when you lose the ego and you merge into this consciousness, then you become one with everything."

Andreas Müller: Yes.

Justin Allen: More like if we were going to say what you're saying, it's more when there is "no one" there, there can't be distinction anymore between me and wall, and that's how maybe you could say, "I'm the wall."

Andreas Müller: Exactly. Yes.

Justin Allen: But you wouldn't be saying you're the wall. You would just really be saying, there actually is no wall as equally as there is "no me," or there is a wall as equally as there is a me. Both are not really happening.

Andreas Müller: Yes. There is nothing that would experience itself as "I'm one with a wall" or something. Yeah. Actually, it's interesting. Well, what I just thought is what you talked about with a child and not knowing. That's also quite a good apparent distinction between I think what spirituality points to and what this message points to. Because I think a lot of spirituality points to the experience of a 4, 5, or 6-year-old child, where there is self-consciousness, whether it's already an experience of "to be," that's why they often sometimes suggest to, "just be." Leave all stories and all knowledge behind you and just be. Enjoy the joy of pure being. That's it exactly what you said about the 4, 5, or 6-year-old child. It looks very innocent because they don't know much. There are not many stories going on. My impression is that the person wants to go back to this innocent experience...

Justin Allen: Yeah. For sure.

Andreas Müller: ...in a way that is this experience of pure being. That's the joy of the innocence...

Justin Allen: Their idea of that experience of pure being.

Andreas Müller: Yeah, exactly. The idea of that. Because there was already an experience in a 4, 5, or 6-year-old child, and it was already accompanied by some unfulfillment, but what this message points to is, so to speak before that works. (before that apparently happens)

Justin Allen: Your message points to the six-month-old or earlier (laughing).

Andreas Müller: Yes, exactly (laughing). Absolutely. Yes. Then there isn't only no knowledge in a conceptual sense, then there is no experience, no self-experience. Yeah.

Justin Allen: That's how you can tell that you're mature. The more mature you are, the younger you want to go back (laughing). I want to go back to being 20 (laughing). That shows my maturity level (as immature). I don't want...

Andreas Müller: Yeah, come on. But that's boring. Everyone wants to be 20 again.

Justin Allen: Yeah. That's why I'm not as mature as you (laughing).

Andreas Müller: Yeah. Yeah. But that's the thing. I'm beyond mature. I'm dead.

Justin Allen: You want to either go to six-months old or even to when... You either want to go to the pre-birth or you want to go to post-life (laughing).

Andreas Müller: But exactly also this with a child, with a 4, 5, or 6-year-old child or the six-month year-old child would also pretty much show the difference between "I don't know" and "no one" there knowing. It's exactly the same thing.

Justin Allen:	You're claiming to be pre-one-year-old, let's say (laughing)?
Andreas Müller:	Well (laughing), I don't really claim it. It's not a goal. It is just like that.
Justin Allen:	Yeah. You're stuck in pre…or post.
Andreas Müller:	They are… Well, in the story… Not really because actually I'm just past life.
Justin Allen:	Yeah. You're pre-life or post-life.
Andreas Müller:	Oh, well.
Justin Allen:	It's the same thing. I mean…
Andreas Müller:	Yeah, in the end, it's the same thing. Yeah. I mean, it's the story.
Justin Allen:	It's like in the story, there's nothing, and then there's something, and then there's nothing again.
Andreas Müller:	So to speak. Yeah. That's what I meant. Exactly. That's the story.
Justin Allen:	You're stuck in nothing now (both laughing).
Andreas Müller:	All right, if that's your story about me, then I'm fine with it (laughing). Yes. I'm helplessly lost in not being someone.
Justin Allen:	Right. But then for you, the reality would be, is that everybody is stuck there as well.
Andreas Müller:	Again?
Justin Allen:	The reality for you in a sense, if you were going to try to describe reality, your attempt to describe reality would put everybody with you in this death

or post-life category or in this "no one's there" category.

Andreas Müller: Yeah. I mean, describing the reality wouldn't even make sense to this concept.

Justin Allen: I know. But I mean, you do attempt to, in a sense, describe what's happening, and when you describe what's happening, what you're saying is that it's not that you are the only one that is post-life. Everybody's post-life.

Andreas Müller: Exactly. The surprise is, so to speak, that what the person would regard as life - nothing, something (meaning: life), nothing - that this something never actually became something. What this message is saying, well, what's a surprise in the end. That it feels like "Oh, I've been born. I know I'm here. Maybe I'm going to die if I won't go on and live forever." But this becoming something never happened. So that's the thing. The difference between nothing and something isn't recognized anymore.

Justin Allen: Right. Then your story in a sense of what is happening, when you're trying to talk about this or describe it, in a sense, you're saying you used to be there and now you're not there anymore. That's why you're referencing yourself as post-life.

Andreas Müller: Yeah. Within that story.

Justin Allen: Yeah, exactly. Within that story. Then let's say that all the people that are listening to you, in their current version of their story, they're in the life version (laughing). But not really. They're also equally in the post-life version that you are in.

Andreas Müller: So to speak. There just is no such thing. This life isn't real. Yes.

Justin Allen:	Right.
Andreas Müller:	Yeah. Yeah. I don't see the difference. People claim to be different by saying, "Well, but I'm here, but I don't..." No matter how often it is claimed, no, I can't confirm that. Let's put it like that. I can't convince anyone otherwise. I don't have an opposite truth, but I can't confirm that.
Justin Allen:	All right.
Andreas Müller:	Yeah.
Justin Allen:	You can't confirm it because I mean, nobody can either, but you admittedly can't confirm it and the difference in general is that people admittedly do confirm it.
Andreas Müller:	Yes, apparently.
Justin Allen:	Yeah. I mean, that's really the only difference, which from where you are, wouldn't be a difference.
Andreas Müller:	Yes.
Justin Allen:	Then if there's a "me" to you, if there's a "me" happening to John or Joe, there's a "me" happening to person A, for you, that's just a leaf falling from a tree or something. It's just what seems to be happening to that person, which isn't really happening.
Andreas Müller:	Yes. Yeah. It's not even really that the illusion is happening like a leaf, but let's put it like this, one body claiming, but "I am person A" is the leaf. Not that there is an additional illusion running, which is the leaf. It's just...
Justin Allen:	But that's what I mean, that's just like a leaf... If I look out the window and a leaf falls from a tree,

then I would say, "Oh, that's happening. The leaf is falling from the tree." If one day I wake up and I seem to be here as a person, then that's what's happening.

Andreas Müller: Yes, absolutely. Yeah.

Justin Allen: Just like that leaf, in a sense, there's nothing that leaf could do about it falling. It couldn't have prevented itself from falling from the tree.

Andreas Müller: Yeah. Yes. Absolutely.

Justin Allen: Just if you think you're there, if that's what's apparently happening that you're there, there's nothing that you (can or could have done about it) ... That's what I mean.

Andreas Müller: Absolutely. Totally. But it's neither right nor wrong, nor true, nor known. Yeah. But it's whole and complete already. Yep.

Justin Allen: Yeah. If it stops, let's say that it ceases to happen, that you think that you were there, as you guys put it, if the "me" falls away... I don't know how you put it. But the "me" falls or whatever, the "me" falls away, that's also what just happened and you didn't do anything to make it happen. Then what you say the surprise is, is that it was always like that, you weren't ever there.

Andreas Müller: Yes. Which can't be explained or it's not logical, but that's the surprise, there already isn't anyone there and there never was. Not that it matters that there never was anyone. It's not important really, but it's a surprise. It was never real. Yeah.

Justin Allen: But even to break, to destroy that word surprise, I think it's not a surprise either. It's just, you're going back in a way to describe it, to communicate it somehow, that's what's happening there and then you're using the word surprise, but it wouldn't be a surprise either. Like what's...

Andreas Müller: Yeah, exactly. Yeah. I mean, of course, the whole idea surprise only works with having an expectation before and stuff like that, but this whole thing drops. You're right, in the end, the natural reality isn't a surprise because it's natural, and in a way, because it always was the case and in that sense you're right. It's actually not a surprise at all.

Justin Allen: It's just an "I don't know moment" (laughing).

Andreas Müller: Well, it's not a moment, but yeah. Yeah.

Justin Allen: It's just "I don't know" then.

Andreas Müller: For no one.

Justin Allen: Yeah. Without a position (laughing). That's all I got. I can beat the dead horse, but...

Andreas Müller: You can?

Justin Allen: There's an expression about beating a dead horse.

Andreas Müller: All right. Okay. I get it. Yeah.

Justin Allen: It's already dead, so there is no need to go on. All right.

Andreas Müller: All right.

Justin Allen: We'll talk some other time.

Andreas Müller: Absolutely. Yeah. I think it was a good idea to do it like that. (Referring to having our first talk of this book *No-Point* without allowing audience feedback)

Justin Allen: Yeah.

Andreas Müller: Yeah.

Justin Allen: It feels better (laughing).

Andreas Müller: Yeah (laughing). For me too. Okay. All right. Thanks, everyone for watching. I hope you, whatever (laughing), enjoyed it (laughing). I don't know. It wasn't for you anyway. Okay.

Justin Allen: Okay.

Andreas Müller: Okay. Thanks, Justin.

Justin Allen: Ciao.

Andreas Müller: Bye. See you. Bye. Thanks.

June 24th, 2021   Talk 19

I WAS NEVER HAPPY BEING ME

Andreas Müller: Okay. All right. So good evening, everyone.
                       Welcome to the live talk with Justin and me. So the
                       idea is that it's our conversation and there are no
                       questions from anyone or stuff like that. So it's just
                       us talking for about an hour, I guess. Okay, just to
                       let you know. All right. I think that's what I wanted
                       to say. And it's being recorded, at least my picture.
                       So you won't be seen. It's just me. (laughing)

Justin Allen: Yeah. I saw there's a warning now, which I think is
                       new for Zoom.

Andreas Müller: That's new. You have to...

Justin Allen: When you record it, then let everybody know you
                       are recording.

Andreas Müller: Yeah. But still it's only me in the picture.

Justin Allen: Okay. All right.

Andreas Müller: So how are you doing?

Justin Allen: Good (laughing). I'm in Los Angeles.

Andreas Müller: All right.

Justin Allen: Not that it matters. So I forgot last time, but I think
                       we talked about, not that it's really relevant, but in

a way the theme or the attempt to have some kind of a theme was surrounded by, "I don't know."

Andreas Müller: Yeah. Yes.

Justin Allen: And I guess in a way to just kind of go into that a bit more, I was thinking about how in your daily life, just from your "no-point perspective," you're just... (laughing)...

Andreas Müller: How daily life is, not knowing anything (laughing).

Justin Allen: Yeah (laughing).

Andreas Müller: To just be blown around the whole day (laughing).

Justin Allen: Right.

Andreas Müller: Uselessly.

Justin Allen: Right. So in a sense, that's really a way of trying to describe it, that's really what it's like. In a sense, there's no planning, although you could say planning might apparently happen, but you couldn't say that there's planning.

Andreas Müller: Yes. True.

Justin Allen: So the way you'd have to say it, is that there's, you'd have to say planning might happen.

Andreas Müller: Apparently in the end, but yes.

Justin Allen: And then while that planning that's apparently happening, it would still just be nothing happening (for you).

Andreas Müller: Yes, absolutely. Not for me, so to speak, but yes.

Justin Allen: All right. And you could retrace at some point later on in the day, you could retrace your steps and say, "Ah, it seemed like that plan happened." Or, "It seemed like I planned an hour ago to be here doing what I'm doing."

Andreas Müller: Whew, I don't know if that would be possible, this experience of retracing, that I could really retrace it. I actually, I don't think so to be honest.

Justin Allen: Wait, I don't mean it necessarily like you're actively retracing, I'm just saying that right now if I said we started this talk five minutes ago.

Andreas Müller: Yes. Okay. Yeah.

Justin Allen: You could say, "Yeah, we planned that and I have it posted on my website, I arranged for all this to happen."

Andreas Müller: Yes, yes.

Justin Allen: So it's a retracing that's happening, that you're actively doing now. That's how we would view it, that you'd actively be able to, but for you, it wouldn't be that you're actively retracing... It would just be that's what's at this moment, it's what's apparently happening is that you're retracing your steps.

Andreas Müller: Yes, absolutely. Yes. It would be effortless. It would just be what happens. And there would be no sense of retracing a real happening, so to speak.

Justin Allen: Right.

Andreas Müller: This would be an experience.

Justin Allen: So in a way, if I were to say that from a perspective, of being here, it would always feel really authentic that I'm actively retracing my steps. If you asked me about my plan or what I did, I would feel like I'm actively doing some kind of "doing" in order to go back and say, "Yeah, that happened and I wanted it to happen that way and I was doing all this planning."

Andreas Müller: Yes. Yeah.

Justin Allen: But in actuality, that sensing of me doing all this stuff is also what's just apparently happening.

Andreas Müller: Yes. One could say so.

Justin Allen: And just to compare those two, if I asked you, "Did we plan to talk two weeks ago on this date?" You would confirm it and say "Yes, of course."

Andreas Müller: Yeah.

Justin Allen: And then I would say, "Did we start talking seven minutes ago?" And you would say, "Yeah, of course."

Andreas Müller: Yeah.

Justin Allen: But even just answering that would be just what's apparently happening.

Andreas Müller: Yes, absolutely.

Justin Allen: And you wouldn't be there doing it, although from a person's perspective, it would seem like you're doing it.

Andreas Müller: Yes.

Justin Allen: And it would also seem logical if we're talking about it in this way that for you to know that you did this two weeks ago and that for you to know that we started talking seven minutes ago, it would mean that you were there all these times to be aware of that and then to reconfirm it now.

Andreas Müller: Yes, absolutely. The person would just project itself into me, so to speak.

Justin Allen: Right. But all those things are still, for you, you'd say they're apparently happening like that answer saying, "Yes, we started talking seven minutes ago." That just is coming out from nothing.

Andreas Müller: Yes, absolutely. Yes.

Justin Allen: And for a person, they feel like it's coming out of something.

Andreas Müller: Exactly. That's their impression. Not that it does come out of something but that's their impression. Yeah.

Justin Allen: But that feeling, so let's say that the answer is coming out and that's what's apparently happening, that feeling that I'm there doing it or remembering or whatever the action is, is also what's apparently happening.

Andreas Müller: Yes.

Justin Allen: So that sense of "me" or that sense of whatever you call it, like the thousand ways that you might call it, the energetic sense of "me" happening or something being there, that's just what's apparently happening to whoever is claiming or feeling that feeling.

Andreas Müller: Yes, so to speak. But actually, not that it really matters, but in the end, I would say it's the illusion of that feeling.

Justin Allen: Right.

Andreas Müller: Because there isn't a real substantial feeling of presence within you that has gone here. The surprise is that it never had any substance, but in the end, yes, this illusory sense to be someone just is what seems to be happening. That you think you are someone and it really feels like that, if that's the case, that's what apparently happens. Yeah.

Justin Allen: Right.

Andreas Müller: Yeah. As much as everything.

Justin Allen: I guess I'm just trying to equalize it. It's the same as when you just said that sentence that you just said, that's the exact same thing in a sense.

Andreas Müller: Yes, totally. It's the exact same "no thing."

Justin Allen: Yeah.

Andreas Müller: Yes, absolutely. Yeah. Totally (both laughing). Yes. That's what I mean actually when I say there's just what seems to be happening and there's no distance or no difference between anyone so to speak or anything in the end.

Justin Allen: Yeah.

Andreas Müller: And yes, the illusion to be someone is what seems to be happening as well as if this apparent illusion doesn't happen.

Justin Allen: It's the same as I'm waving my hand now, that's what's apparently happening. And then if there's a sensed self of me waving my hand, that's also what's apparently happening.

Andreas Müller: Yes. Yes. In a way, one could say the person's problem is that it's already wholeness.

Justin Allen: Yeah.

Andreas Müller: If it would be real, it would have something to work on and to overcome and all those things, but it's not something different in the first place.

Justin Allen: And just like if I wave my hand and then I stop waving my hand, that just apparently happened that I stopped waving my hand.

Andreas Müller: Yeah.

Justin Allen: And if the sensed self or the sensed "me" is no longer apparently happening, or the illusion is no longer being illusory (laughing).

Andreas Müller: Being seemingly real you mean (laughing).

Justin Allen: Right. Seemingly real. That would just be the same as how my hand was just stopped waving that it just...

Andreas Müller: Kind of, yep.

Justin Allen: Basically, arbitrarily discontinued (my hand waving), although all that's weird to talk about because you can't say discontinued now that you just said that it's not happening in the first place.

Andreas Müller: Yeah. That would be the simplified picture of this, of liberation.

Justin Allen: So, at some point in the book (*No-Point Perspective*) we were talking about how, if all the stuff, I think there's this point where we're talking about how if all of a sudden you walked outside and there were, dinosaurs walking around again.

Andreas Müller: Yeah.

Justin Allen: For you, that wouldn't be remarkable (laughing). You can't know for sure, but...

Andreas Müller:	It would just be an ordinary day of wholeness (laughing).
Justin Allen:	Right.
Andreas Müller:	Maybe I wouldn't even recognize.
Justin Allen:	Right. Or if the book *Metamorphosis*, like if you woke up and you were an insect.
Andreas Müller:	Yeah (laughing).
Justin Allen:	Nothing would've changed for you (laughing).
Andreas Müller:	Yes (laughing). Kind of (laughing). There's just no real "I" or "you."
Justin Allen:	Right. There wouldn't be a dilemma. The dilemma for a person would be is if they woke up as an insect, might be, "Oh damn, now I'm an insect (laughing)."
Andreas Müller:	Yeah, exactly. It would suddenly become aware that, oh, exactly as you said, "Oh fuck, I'm an insect."
Justin Allen:	Right.
Andreas Müller:	And it would quickly remember the story of karma and then try to retrace how all of this happened (laughing).
Justin Allen:	Right. Or whatever. It doesn't have to be karma. It could be whatever the... (Whatever is referring to the person maybe not blaming it on karma, but instead on, "What did I do wrong in life, that it turned me into an insect"?)
Andreas Müller:	Yeah. Yeah, of course.

Justin Allen:	It would try to come up with a reason for why it's happening and then how to get back to pre-insect "me," if insect-me wasn't preferred. People might prefer being the insect. But for you then, in this sense, there wouldn't be any dilemma.
Andreas Müller:	Yes (laughing). It might be apparently weird, but yes. And there's just now... It's always difficult to say for you it would be like this because there just isn't a real for you.
Justin Allen:	But that's what I mean by that, I just mean, there wouldn't... Like you could still wake up and think, "Oh look, I don't have an arm anymore. I have a leg where my arm used to be."
Andreas Müller:	Yes.
Justin Allen:	I don't know what the body parts of insects are (laughing). You have a wing instead or something.
Andreas Müller:	Yeah.
Justin Allen:	So it would be a shock. It could be shocking to you.
Andreas Müller:	Exactly.
Justin Allen:	But there wouldn't be this strong attachment that this is happening to something or someone.
Andreas Müller:	Yes. Kind of. It's just a bit difficult because it seems to create a difference between again, between "me" and anyone, but that difference isn't real, but I know what you're trying to get at. Yes. There just wouldn't be in that sense this self-experience and all the consequences out of that. But it may sound much more different than it is because this "I" experience and self-consequences, they never really happened even when there is/was "someone," but I can't explain that. This whole

sense of "I am" and all the stories and stuff, they are so much not on the foreground of everyone's life. Seen from the person it feels as if it's constantly about "me" and my life and my story, but it actually in anyone's life, this is never really the case. The "I" is never really in the foreground.

Justin Allen: Yeah.

Andreas Müller: Finally, amazingly.

Justin Allen: When we talked at some point when we were in the earlier conversations, I was trying to understand what it's like for you. And you get asked, this is a typical question, everybody's curious about what it was like before for you and what it was/is like after, even though the reality is there was no before and there is no after. But when somebody's trying to understand that, and then you said this (one particular) sentence that has stuck with me, you said that it was easier for you to be you. So let's just make...

Andreas Müller: All right. Yeah. I know what you mean.

Justin Allen: Making a point (as a concession), let's say that you were living your life as a "me" and then all of a sudden you weren't.

Andreas Müller: Yes.

Justin Allen: And then I was trying to understand what that was like. And you said, one of the sentences that has stuck with me, is something like, "The funny thing is, I actually felt more comfortable being me." (You felt more comfortable being "me" after the "me" disappeared)

Andreas Müller: Yes, totally. Absolutely. Yes.

Justin Allen:	And the way that I've interpreted that, because in the book (*No-Point Perspective*) I don't think we talked about that further and I felt like I understood what you meant at the time, but the way that I would paraphrase your meaning about that was that, before, you weren't comfortable being "me" (being yourself in the sense that you were constantly trying to update or upgrade or improve yourself or change or modify or do something). And then when the "me" dropped away, then you could, if you like to eat, if you like to go to this, if you wanted to study this particular course or do this particular thing, maybe you stopped yourself before because you thought it wasn't in line with some other ("me") direction. And now because there wasn't this, "me" interference or this energetic interference, that that's the liberation in the sense that you could just be yourself, not that you're actively being yourself, but then it could just happen.
Andreas Müller:	Exactly. Yes. One could say so, absolutely. I think this happens for most people (that most people are not fully happy being themselves) actually to some degree, I was never happy being Andreas. In a way I was quite confident being an "I," but I was quite unsatisfied that this "I" was Andreas (laughing).
Justin Allen:	Right (laughing).
Andreas Müller:	So yes, so I constantly tried. That was this constant struggle in a way, because I experienced Andreas from a separate standpoint and immediately it was part of that which wasn't enough. Andreas already was experienced as it's not whole, it's not everything. And yes, and I tried to work on myself, so to speak, for a while. I wasn't working on having a career. I wasn't working on having, I don't know, power or whatever someone can work on.

Andreas Müller:

I was working on my conditioning (correcting my conditioning), at least for a while partly, having fun, working on my conditioning, become a better Andreas, whatever I thought this would look like. Yeah, absolutely. And yes, whether when the person dropped, it turned out that Andreas too was wholeness or was just naturally fine. And there was in that sense no conflict anymore. Not that it was replaced by a miraculous state of acceptance. There is nothing in here knowing that I'm good or okay or totally accepted. I don't even need a story about myself being okay. I have no idea. I don't regard myself as good and okay. But when the person dropped, this inner struggle with myself, so to speak, or with this body dropped.

Justin Allen:

Right. And that's generally always a subtle distinction between, your message and Disney Worlds or Hollywood or gurus or awareness teachings or therapy or whatever. That's just generally the general distinction is that they might say a similar thing occurred. They might say that I was struggling all the time and then when I awoke or whatever, then I was finally free and comfortable to just be how I am or to just be me. That would be their sentence.

Andreas Müller:

Yeah. Yeah. But my impression is that's rather a claim.

Justin Allen:

That's what I'm saying. That's the subtle distinction.

Andreas Müller:

Yes. Yes. I mean the Hollywood...

Justin Allen:

You're taking away the authorship and you're taking away the claim, you're taking away that something's there then to go about life freely and to just enjoy it now because there's no longer this energetic interference.

Andreas Müller:	Yes. Yeah. In the Hollywood movie, they usually end when the people (laughing) at that point where it's said, "Well, now all is fine." So usually the film ends at that, but in a spiritual teaching, there may be this claim. But if you look closer, it remains within a method. So usually it's, "Well, the moment I realized who I really am, a lot of struggle fell away, or since then I'm on a path of loving myself." But if you look closer, there is always still a method going on. It's a lifelong integration. It's a lifelong path of acceptance and stuff like that.
Justin Allen:	And it's still a clear authorship.
Andreas Müller:	Yes, absolutely. But to the sense of authorship, there is a doing attached still.
Justin Allen:	Right.
Andreas Müller:	Because the general picture is when this claim is made, there is this aura of I've done it, I've reached it and after that, it's effortless or something. But if you look closer, it never is. That's what I mean. Because there is still a kind of a path, a process, a concept, a method attached to it.
Justin Allen:	It made me think of the ugly, I don't know if I have the right fairytale, but *The Ugly Duckling*, I think. And it's where, if I remember correctly, I think it's a goose that ends up in a duck family or something like that.
Andreas Müller:	All right. I don't... Okay.
Justin Allen:	I'm pretty sure (laughing). I think it's a baby goose somehow is adopted into a duck family.
Andreas Müller:	All right (laughing).

Justin Allen:	So it doesn't fit in as a baby because it looks weird to all the other ducklings and it can't do the same things and it doesn't have the same nature as all the other ducklings. And so it gets kind of outcasted or treated as an outsider the whole time. And it itself is having the dilemma of trying to be something that it's not.
Andreas Müller:	Mm, okay. All right.
Justin Allen:	That's the general plot. And then at some point it grows up and it turns into this beautiful white goose, I guess. And then comes the fairytale part where then it realizes that it was beautiful all the time or something.
Andreas Müller:	Yeah. Yeah.
Justin Allen:	But to me, what I thought was interesting...
Andreas Müller:	It's one of those stories that tries to make people feel good about themselves (laughing).
Justin Allen:	Exactly. Or yeah, for the outsider to understand that it has its own beauty, somewhere.
Andreas Müller:	Yeah. Everyone has tears in their eyes because, well, yeah. Yeah.
Justin Allen:	But the point about it in a way that I could relate to what you were saying is that, and even this is filled with contradiction or it's not clean enough to say, but if you were a goose... if you're trying to fight your goose nature to be a duck, that's just obvious that's going to be a big conflict.
Andreas Müller:	Yes.
Justin Allen:	And you could say the same in a way, if you're trying to be a "me" when there's not even a "me" that exists, that's going to be conflict. And then if you

just say that sentence, then somebody of course hearing that would go, "Oh fuck, I don't want to be a 'me,' then all I have to do is get rid of this 'me'." And then you're in the loop or you're, in a sense you're just perpetuating the false-meaning.

Andreas Müller: Yes. Because in a funny way, you again are fighting against what seems to be happening.

Justin Allen: Right.

Andreas Müller: You're again trying to become something which you aren't, so to speak.

Justin Allen: Exactly. You just lock yourself into a more difficult maze in a sense. Not that you are there to do it, but that seems to be what then is happening in that space.

Andreas Müller: Yeah, it's equally difficult I would say.

Justin Allen: Yeah.

Andreas Müller: But I know it seems more impossible, but it's actually equally impossible or equally difficult. But yeah, I know what you mean.

Justin Allen: So anyways, everybody is like that to some degree. As long as there's a "me," there's that automatic, "I'm not good enough," or, "I don't fit in," or, "Something's missing."

Andreas Müller: Or, "I have to do something." Yeah, yeah.

Justin Allen: And it's just like the goose or it's just like a squirrel being raised by rats or something, it would never fit in and it would never be able to have the same... When it compared itself, it would never be the same. And it would never feel satisfied or fulfilled because it's just not fitting in.

Andreas Müller: Yeah, it will never become the other whatever. Yeah.

Justin Allen: And you can actively see that if you know species, you can actively see, yeah, of course it's never going to work because you're not a duck. And in a sense, that's your message, you're going, of course to everybody, it's never going to work. None of this is going to work because you're not a "me," you're not a person. (If you are not a "me" in the first place or ever, but you are trying to escape being this non-me "me," which isn't even happening, you are in a sense the goose trying to be the duck.)

Andreas Müller: Yes. Yeah.

Justin Allen: So, the huge dilemma in a sense is obvious in the fairy tales with the animals and the different species. And in this case (the "me" case), it's impossible to diagnose or treat or do anything with because it's by definition to be in the problem (the "me" problem, which isn't really a problem), there already has to be the illusion of a "me" happening.

Andreas Müller: Yes, absolutely. Yeah.

Justin Allen: And then automatically, if there's a "me," it's automatically not going to feel like it fits in and it's going to struggle to change. I'm just using the word fit in. It's going to try to adjust or modify.

Andreas Müller: Yeah, exactly. Yeah.

Justin Allen: And so, if there is no "me" though, then in a sense you can then be comfortable being a "me." (Or letting an apparent "me" happen as it happens.)

Andreas Müller: Again? If there is no "me" ...

Justin Allen: If there is no "me," then you can be... It's going to sound controversial (laughing). If there is no "me," then you can be comfortable being a "me."

Andreas Müller: Yes and no. Theoretically, yes, absolutely. But practically to be a "me" means to be uncomfortable.

Justin Allen: Yeah. But you know what I mean? (Andreas confirms with a "Totally") That's what your sentence was saying is that after the "me" died, you could be comfortable being Andreas finally.

Andreas Müller: Yes. Yeah, yeah. But it's actually we talked about this a little bit because even in a way, theoretically, but that's impossible, one can even be comfortable in being a "me" and seeking and stuff like that. That's also already whole and complete. It won't become the person's experience.

Justin Allen: Right. But in theory you could keep on ... let's say that you're no longer a "me," there's nothing there anymore. It could still happen that searching happens.

Andreas Müller: That's the thing, it depends on what you would regard as searching.

Justin Allen: Yeah. Hopefully I'm talking about the searching (laughing) that doesn't involve a "me" to search...

Andreas Müller: Yeah, so to speak, seeking my keys or finding a solution for a problem, so to speak.

Justin Allen: Exactly.

Andreas Müller: And the person would see, "Oh, well he's also seeking," but there wouldn't be the seeking setup. That's the only thing that I would regard as seeking.

Justin Allen: Right.

Andreas Müller:	Someone seeking fulfillment in what happened or happens.
Justin Allen:	Right. But there's actual seeking going on and it's like you're searching for a new house or if you're searching for...
Andreas Müller:	Yes, exactly. And there might be...
Justin Allen:	It might happen that you don't like where you live and you want to move to someplace else.
Andreas Müller:	Absolutely. There might be obstacles. They need papers. I have to run around to the locals, to the townhouse and get papers and it's closed when I arrive and all that crap, so to speak.
Justin Allen:	Right.
Andreas Müller:	That may be, yes, oh totally, of course. But it wouldn't be experienced as I'm seeking; I'm doing that in order to gain fulfillment.
Justin Allen:	Right. It wouldn't be fraught...
Andreas Müller:	What apparently...
Justin Allen:	It wouldn't be fraught with "me" problems and it would be just naturally occurring, whereas in the sense when there's the "me" there, it's kind of the way that you talk about it, is it's an un-natural, everything that comes out of it automatically is un-natural in the sense that the sense of "me" is already not happening.
Andreas Müller:	I didn't get that.
Justin Allen:	If it's already impossible to talk about because there's not a "me" happening in the first place.

Andreas Müller:	Yeah. In a way it is like that for everyone also. It's not that it exclusively is for me that it's just what seems to be happening. It's like that for everyone, so to speak.
Justin Allen:	Right.
Andreas Müller:	But when there is the illusion of a person, there is the assumption that all of this, me wanting a bigger house, me having to go to the townhouse, organizing the papers, that it is somehow happening for me or because of me that it somehow is part of my journey towards fulfillment.
Justin Allen:	Right.
Andreas Müller:	That dream that drops.
Justin Allen:	And because of that, then that's automatically in that kind of a happening, it's fraught with what you would call or generally we would all call conflict and dilemmas. And I'm talking about the internal "me" dilemmas, not the...
Andreas Müller:	Yes. Yes.
Justin Allen:	External dilemma of having to go to the town and court and bank.
Andreas Müller:	Yeah.
Justin Allen:	So that's, to me, that's again going back to previous conversations and everything, that's also how it's so ordinary going back to that word or how it's all still the same. And that was kind of shocking to me or I guess it wasn't that shocking, but when we were first talking and you get a sense of how regular and normal you are (non-guru-like).
Andreas Müller:	Yeah (laughing), it doesn't look like I know, but yes. Yeah, yeah.

Justin Allen: But you start off in general with thinking how different it must be for you.

Andreas Müller: Yes, absolutely.

Justin Allen: Yeah, and at the same time, it is, it's dramatic, you could say it's dramatically different, but equally it's un-dramatic, it's such a simple or such a subtle distinction.

Andreas Müller: Yeah.

Justin Allen: To be there or not be there.

Andreas Müller: Yeah. One can't really...

Justin Allen: Everything is exactly the same.

Andreas Müller: Yeah. Yeah. One can't really point the finger on the difference and say, "Well, that's the difference. There it is." Because yeah, it's not real. Yeah.

Justin Allen: And it's also kind of like, let's say that if you're going about your day, even though you wouldn't say this, if there's a "me" happening, it's there and you could say there's degrees. It seems like some people there's more "me-ness" happening than others, right?

Andreas Müller: Yeah. I think we, yeah, that's a tough one.

Justin Allen: But it seems like it.

Andreas Müller: All right (not really sure or willing to fully confirm).

Justin Allen: Somebody that's neurotic and worried about everything, it seems like there's a stronger, let's say it is energetic. If it is energetic, they seem to have more of an energetic need (laughing).

Andreas Müller:	Yeah (laughing). A more troubled "me" for whatever reason. Yes.
Justin Allen:	Right.
Andreas Müller:	Yeah. I know what you mean. Yeah.
Justin Allen:	Then for that person, if all of a sudden that or they disappeared, to them it might be a more dramatic change or to them they might think, "Wow, before I was so stressed and my body was tight and worried all the time." (Andreas confirms) And then somebody that wasn't so energetically lost or whatever you call it, for them it might be almost nothing. It might be just a, "I used to go to the refrigerator and I would kind of think that I was going to the refrigerator to get my glass of milk and now it's clear, I'm not going to the refrigerator anymore to get my glass of milk."
Andreas Müller:	...(laughing) Yes. I know what you mean. I think what happens for a lot of people is that when they have an awakening, apparently, they have been a "me" for all their life and suddenly there is a hole (emptiness). Out of nothing, so to speak. For some people, this is quite dramatic. And my story to this is that there is such an intense contrast happening.
Justin Allen:	Yeah.
Andreas Müller:	Hmm.
Justin Allen:	But if you go to a daily thing, like you go to brush your teeth, a person might say, "Oh yeah, I have to go brush my teeth." That could turn into a dilemma of where the person could have an argument like, "Oh, I don't want to get up and go brush my teeth."
Andreas Müller:	Yeah. I want to lay down and yeah, yeah.

Justin Allen:	And then it comes in and goes, "Well, I have to, it's really important." And you have the whole discussion about it.
Andreas Müller:	Yeah.
Justin Allen:	And then you get up and you go brush your teeth and then you have to stand there for a few minutes. And while you're standing there for a few minutes, you could be, totally in your head thinking, "Oh, this is so boring." Or you're brushing a certain way to switch up the routine. So, it's not like you (laughing) start here and then you move over to here and all that stuff is actively going on.
Andreas Müller:	I can't remember having brushed my teeth so consciously (laughing) even when I was a "me" (laughing). Yeah, sorry. Yeah.
Justin Allen:	And then if that's kind of the regular business and then all of a sudden you start brushing your teeth and you're not really having this whole dialogue going on, although you still might be brushing one side and randomly moving all around. So even in that story or in that setup, there's no difference almost. It's such a subtle difference.
Andreas Müller:	Yes. Yeah.
Justin Allen:	And I was thinking about how the reality is that there's "no one" there, but then it seems like that someone's there for a lot of people.
Andreas Müller:	Yes. That's what seems to be happening, yeah.
Justin Allen:	Yeah. But even though while it seems like that's what's happening, it's not really happening.
Andreas Müller:	Yes. But this can't be...

Justin Allen:	Yeah. And the thing that I wanted to get to is that you can't recognize it.
Andreas Müller:	True. Yeah.
Justin Allen:	And then you never recognize it at any point. You say, "Something shifted and then there's no longer a 'me'." As soon as that happens, there's not anything there to even register or recognize that there was that change or that happened.
Andreas Müller:	Yes, absolutely. Yes. You're right. Yeah, it doesn't make sense anymore.
Justin Allen:	And so, in a way it goes unnoticed. You know what I mean?
Andreas Müller:	Yeah. Totally. There is just, not even it goes unnoticed, this whole setup of noticing something turns out to be illusory.
Justin Allen:	Right.
Andreas Müller:	But it's really impossible to explain that, how what that is, how that actually really is. I can't explain that.
Justin Allen:	And that's what I was driving towards is that (laughing) thing that you just said you can't talk about (laughing).
Andreas Müller:	That was kind of an approach, yes. Yeah.
Justin Allen:	Because the way that I was trying to do it with all those (set-ups), like that previous whole setup was just to say, you could just never recognize it.
Andreas Müller:	Yes.
Justin Allen:	So it's actually the case. It's literally actually the

	case that you're not there, that there's nothing there.
Andreas Müller:	Or anyone.
Justin Allen:	Right.
Andreas Müller:	Yeah.
Justin Allen:	But somehow you think that there is someone there, and that is a recognition. Just automatically that is already a recognition, which isn't really happening.
Andreas Müller:	That is the apparent recognition, yes. And that's the only moment so to speak when the setup of noticing starts.
Justin Allen:	Yeah.
Andreas Müller:	That is noticing, recognition of something happening, noticing of something. Yeah.
Justin Allen:	And then when that illusion seems to happen, then you recognize that you don't like it or that you don't want to be it or that you want to get out or that you're the goose in the duck family setup. And so, then the only way that you can get out of it would be to recognize something else that's not it, which you can't do. (Because there is "no one" there in the first place to do something.)
Andreas Müller:	Yeah.
Justin Allen:	You know what I mean? Because the only way would be then, is to become enlightened or to become awakened or to...
Andreas Müller:	Another thing that one can notice.

Justin Allen:	Right.
Andreas Müller:	That's the only thing that makes sense within that setup. Whatever my fulfillment looks like, whatever the answer is, it must be something that I can notice again.
Justin Allen:	And it's different from what I'm currently experiencing and aware of.
Andreas Müller:	Absolutely. Because this isn't it. What I notice now definitely isn't it. The "I" doesn't even have to think about that. This impression that that's not it in a way comes before I'm able to think about it. It's instantly happening together with the noticing, with a becoming aware of oneself. And you're right, the only thing that makes sense is it must be something, my fulfillment must be something that I can notice on the one hand and it still has to come because this isn't it.
Justin Allen:	Yeah.
Andreas Müller:	Yes.
Justin Allen:	That's the impossibility of it because you won't ever find it. Right (rhetorically)? And you can't ever change because there's not something there that can change or that can find something else anyways.
Andreas Müller:	Yes.
Justin Allen:	So, I don't know even how to word this, but that's what I wanted to try to talk about more to somehow stoke the flame, was that you can't recognize it. And that to me, if you were really trying to talk about the problem (laughing), that's the way you'd have to talk about the problem is that you're trying to recognize it and just by that trying (to recognize)

is already, it's like you're denying, it's an act of denying that you're already (not recognizable or not there) ... Yeah.

Andreas Müller:

That's the funny thing. All the person's effort and hopes are on recognizing something, but recognizing something doesn't have any value at all. It doesn't play a role in what we talk about here. Seen from the person that's the only thing it has, so to speak, to recognize, to be, it's what it consists of and what it seeks in and it just doesn't matter. It has nothing... The end of itself or fulfillment or stuff like that has in that sense nothing to do with any kind of recognition or experience or knowing. Yeah. And the sense of recognition is the illusion.

Justin Allen:

Right.

Andreas Müller:

It's not that there is a real illusion that one has to overcome and see through. No, it's just the self-experience, the recognized, noticing something. Yeah.

Justin Allen:

Then I was trying to use the toothbrush or going to the refrigerator, like a mundane action, a mundane, daily task in a way.

Andreas Müller:

Sorry (laughing), but going to the refrigerator can be a task (laughing)?

Justin Allen:

A what (laughing)?

Andreas Müller:

I just found it funny to call walking to the refrigerator a task.

Justin Allen:

Yeah. It can be work, getting up to go to the refrigerator.

Andreas Müller:

I understand if one has already the brushing the teeth problem, then going to the refrigerator, oh sorry, I'm joking.

Justin Allen: But you know what I mean, going to the refrigerator is a mundane, trivial thing that might happen in a day, to go to the refrigerator to get fruit or to get a glass of whatever. And for a super conscious person, they might be aware of everything that they're doing of how they might put their hand on the handle and how they open the door. And you can see it in texts of Zen or guru teachers, there's that whole art of Zen where you put your mind into everything and so everything's a graceful act or that's the extreme version. Or being mindful of everything.

Andreas Müller: Yeah.

Justin Allen: But still, generally everybody that's going to the refrigerator, let's just assume that in such a mundane activity, there's still somebody there doing it.

Andreas Müller: Yeah, at least that's the illusion. Yeah.

Justin Allen: Right. But we can accept it in a lot of cases in the daily life of a person, they're "not there" all the time. They're turning on a faucet or they're picking up something from the floor or they're just sitting there and they're "not there." They're not actively there. But when they are actively there opening up a refrigerator and then all of a sudden one day, they get up to open the refrigerator and they're "not there" doing it anymore, but still the refrigerator is getting opened and they're still grabbing something from it. And they might even still be thinking something about the thing that they're grabbing, or they might think about how they opened up the refrigerator, but they're "not there" doing it anymore. Even though those thoughts might still be happening, feelings might still be happening, an action happening. But there's just the lacking of "me" (or recognition) behind it all. And that wouldn't be recognizable.

Andreas Müller:	Yes. One could say so, yes. Yep.
Justin Allen:	Now it's getting, maybe kind of philosophical, but if you don't recognize it (the "me") anymore, that all of a sudden you don't recognize what you're doing, then you might think... It's impossible to talk about, but if it wasn't recognizable, you wouldn't think anything happened. And because you were your whole time so focused on thinking something had to happen or something, I know this isn't true, but it's almost like you could kind of say that it's like blocking yourself from (blocking yourself from "no-me") (laughing)... You can't say it, but you know what I mean. It's like, you're blocking yourself. It might happen every single day and it's like you miss it because it's so subtle, because you think something has to be recognized, something has to change.
Andreas Müller:	Because there's nothing to be seen. Because it's not that you miss it because it's so subtle. No, because there's nothing to be seen actually.
Justin Allen:	And because you're so actively expecting or somehow thinking that something has to be seen.
Andreas Müller:	Yeah. Absolutely. But only when the person's back. In that moment, it's not really a misunderstanding because you're expecting something else. Because in the moment when there are no wonders, of course also no expectation running. It actually kicks in again when the person comes back.
Justin Allen:	But because it's so... Instantly if it's unrecognizable, that's the most foreign thing to a "me."
Andreas Müller:	Totally (excitedly). That is such a weird idea that, yeah, that there's nothing to be recognized. That's the weirdest idea for a person.

Justin Allen:	Yeah. So let's just say that it was simple to talk about and discuss and to point out, if there was a strategy or something to figuring this out, the person you could say, if you were trying to communicate this to people, you'd have to somehow say it's so obvious or it's just clearly that there's nothing there, but because you're so actively trying to see that something's there and that's the only thing that you can basically grasp as something that's graspable. Because it's not graspable, you can't see it. You can't do anything about it.
Andreas Müller:	But it would be totally useless information again.
Justin Allen:	Yeah. True.
Andreas Müller:	Kind of. I just had a funny thought, well funny, about the Zen guy going to the fridge. The thing is even when there is "no one" and suddenly the person comes back, there of course can be a recognition of, "Oh, where have I been? Now I'm back again." Stuff like that. But for the seeker, this would even feel dangerous or not acceptable. The seeker would turn this into something that's (really) wrong actually. Not having been there. I think everyone knows that in a way, like a time when there really wasn't anything going on and suddenly you are like, "Oh, whoa, whoa, what?" (And panic might set in – existential panic) Not a big thing mostly, just this subtle impression, "Hey, I'm back. I'm here. What happened? I don't know what…" Stuff like that. But for the spiritual seeker in their story, this would actually be labeled as bad, not having been there, a wasted moment without presence, a wasted moment having missed the possibility of becoming enlightened, stuff like that.
Justin Allen:	Yeah.
Andreas Müller:	But I think even most people, I think most people who live in this story of I'm a conscious "me,"

usually they're on a path of becoming more and more conscious. I think hardly anyone would regard themselves as, "I'm constantly conscious all the time." It usually remains a path or an ideal. So I think every one of them knows the moments when they aren't conscious. On the one hand, just because they are lost in stories, which is regarded as wrong. But I think they also know those moments when there was nothing, which no one knows, but this subtle coming back into being "me." I think most people know this too in a way. Then there is always a sense of fear, something was wrong, where have I been? I should have been there actually. I missed something.

Justin Allen: But that's the thing, let's say that I'm a "me" and I'm going about trying to unbecome "me."

Andreas Müller: Yeah. Sorry, one sentence. And in those moments, it's in the end not even missed that there was wholeness, it's even turned wrong. It's even turned into something that's wrong actually (laughing).

Justin Allen: That's what I wanted to say is that if I'm a "me" and I'm trying to unbecome "me" and I've done many things, like I've done all the things and now I've landed into some spiritual teacher, some spiritual path let's say, and I've done different spiritual paths and now I've finally found the right one or whatever. And then this path that I'm on tells me that I should meditate or that I should be conscious of everything or whatever it might tell me. But one day while I'm on the spiritual path, I go to the refrigerator and I'm not there for a moment. And I come back and it's not desirable that I wasn't there because it didn't give me anything. Right? And it didn't give me anything because there was "no me" there to give or to get anything.

Andreas Müller: Yes.

Justin Allen:	And I don't profit from it in any way. There was no amazing experience. There was no relaxation that happened. There was nothing.
Andreas Müller:	Yes.
Justin Allen:	So coming out of that, the "me" comes back, the "me" wouldn't think necessarily like, "Oh, that was it." But the coming back to being a "me" again after not being a "me" might then reconfirm the "me" and might give you a sense, like, "Oh, something happened there." Because you disappeared, let's say it disappeared for a second.
Andreas Müller:	Yeah. But the person would usually just turn it into another story, I've been unconscious or it usually...
Justin Allen:	I'm just saying, whatever they might turn into, some story or otherwise and then they might think, or they might even think that was an enlightening moment or something happened to them where they had an experience so they seek after it. But still, that's why I was trying to say, is if you could say that, let's just pretend that all you have to do as a seeker is when there's a moment that you're not there and you just stay there in that moment... (laughing)
Andreas Müller:	No, that's too much of a contradiction.
Justin Allen:	I know (laughing), but let's just say that you could.
Andreas Müller:	Okay.
Justin Allen:	You could just stay there. And that was the trick, let's say.
Andreas Müller:	Yeah.
Justin Allen:	That person would never want to do it anyways

because it still thinks that there has to be an experience or there has to be something happening for it.

Andreas Müller: Yes. It's not really logical because of course let's say liberation would be a personal thing or let's say you could stay in that moment, then of course the need for something else would be also gone.

Justin Allen: Yeah.

Andreas Müller: So in that sense, there wouldn't be the discarding of it because it would be wholeness then.

Justin Allen: I guess I'm just trying to say it in a way of you can't...

Andreas Müller: I know what you mean.

Justin Allen: You can't recognize it and you think that you have to recognize it and that's the only thing that you're interested in, even though in a day, in a 24-hour day, there were multiple periods in that day where you weren't there, it wouldn't mean anything to you because it was so un-experiential.

Andreas Müller: Absolutely.

Justin Allen: Yes.

Andreas Müller: It wouldn't mean anything. Totally. Yes.

Justin Allen: And that's why it's almost like, then you could almost start to say sentences like, the harder you seek or the more you seek or the more you try to be conscious, even though this isn't true, it's almost in a sense like you're decreasing your chances of the illusion dropping. (not that there is an illusion in the first place)

Andreas Müller:

Yes. Kind of. Well, yeah, I know what you mean. Yes. But not really because death can happen out of any position, but in a way, one could say - not as a real process - like you are decreasing the possibility or stuff, but the actual trying to be conscious is confirming the separation in this instance, so to speak, not necessarily in a longer process or something. But of course, the moment you seek, you are separate and you are seeking, so to speak. Yeah.

Justin Allen:

This is totally not relevant and it's also not true, but I feel like saying it, is that you can start to see a logic to this idea of meditating in a way or of kind of doing nothing let's say. In one sense, you can't understand it because you're still giving somebody something to do and they're doing this...

Andreas Müller:

Exactly.

Justin Allen:

Expecting something to come out of it. But at the same time, it's like, you're trying to get enlightened by climbing up to the top of the mountain or something. And it's this action where you have a goal and you're trying to get there. Or you are supposed to do your job and work and have a family and you're busy with all those things all the time so you're occupied and your mind's busy and active and everything's active. And then somebody comes along and says here's meditation. And the hope in a way is that while you're just sitting there, everything's busy, that somehow the "me" falls away or that it could all of a sudden disappear, but you know what I mean? There's a logic to that. How did humans invent this idea of meditation?

Andreas Müller:

Well, yeah, of course. Oh yeah, yeah, of course. But it would still be a personal invention.

Justin Allen:

Right.

Andreas Müller: And of course, in all personal ideas is logic. The person's methods, it's not that they are illogical. They are pure logic. They can very clearly explain why you have to do this, what's the purpose of this, and what's the supposed outcome.

Justin Allen: Yeah.

Andreas Müller: Actually, you find that of course. Within the personal paradigm, every teaching makes perfect sense.

Justin Allen: Yeah.

Andreas Müller: And not only from logic, but because it can seemingly be experienced. So if you think a silent mind, so to speak, leads to liberation, the idea of meditation makes perfect sense. And you can even experience that your mind gets calmer for a while.

Justin Allen: Yeah, exactly. And it might be healthy. It might actually be physically healthy for the human body to meditate just like you can argue it's healthy for the human body to eat well and it's healthy to climb up the mountain and come back down again.

Andreas Müller: Whatever. Exactly. So within the person's story, all those ideas and beliefs and methods, they make perfect sense.

Justin Allen: Yeah.

Andreas Müller: I think that's something which even confirms the person that it is logical, it must be true to some degree. That's something that makes it even more valid for the person.

Justin Allen: Yeah. We talked about this too in the book (*No-Point Perspective*) where, if I was a seeker and I tried a bunch of different things (to escape) and then I went off to a meditation retreat for one month, and on the 10th day, the "me" dropped away. Now for me, if the "me" dropped away, let's say it truly authentically dropped away, I wouldn't say that it was because of meditation.

Andreas Müller: Yes. Absolutely.

Justin Allen: But, all the people that knew that I went there and if there was a leader of this meditation camp and it was confirmed officially like I got my (enlightenment) stamp...

Andreas Müller: (laughing)...But the leader of the meditation camp wouldn't be able to confirm that because she or he would have no idea what you are talking about (laughing).

Justin Allen: Yeah. Let's just say that she did (laughing). For her business, it's good that every once in a while, every... (few years someone gets enlightened)

Andreas Müller: Somewhat, yeah. Okay (laughing). All right.

Justin Allen: Every 10 or 20 years somebody shouts, "I'm not there anymore." Then all the people there and that would hear the story could think and assume that it's because I was meditating.

Andreas Müller: Yes, totally. Of course.

Justin Allen: And then same with somebody that goes to, they say they went to India and they traveled around for 10 years and somewhere in there their "me" dropped, then everybody thinks they have to go to India or something.

Andreas Müller: It's this question, I often get this question saying, "but you were also, Andreas, you were also a seeker, a spiritual seeker, so isn't there a connection?" But of course, it's a story that it's usually presented by

all the gurus. So it's not really that the people...
I think this idea rather doesn't come from talking
about "me" and my story, but it's just a story
that teachers and gurus and stuff present since
hundreds of years, or the person experiencing
presents this story since hundreds of years. You
have to do this, there is a path, blah blah blah. So
that the seeker has to think this, that something
happened to me because of my path.

Justin Allen: But to me, I know you've said this a thousand times,
but it's in a way, for lack of a better way of saying it,
it's like I understand what you mean if you say it's
not recognizable, or you'll never get it. That always
had different meanings to me when you said it. But
it's really... I'm repeating it because it makes so
much sense, but it's hard to then talk further about
it, even though I want to, somehow, I want to find
another way to talk about it. But there's something
so interesting about how it's unrecognizable and
how just in everything that you're doing throughout
the day, you're actually never there.

Andreas Müller: Yes. And in a funny way, that is the attraction
because that is the freedom. And as you say, when
there is "no one," it's not really, what was the word
that you were saying? Mystical? No, you didn't say
mystical.

Justin Allen: I was saying unrecognizable (laughing).

Andreas Müller: Yeah, no, but you said something like interesting
or fantastic or something like that, I don't know. I
forgot.

Justin Allen: I don't know either.

Andreas Müller: But that is the interesting thing that on the one
hand you can't talk about it, you can't go there.
On the other hand, exactly that's the freedom and

that's also the attraction, the apparent attraction of this message.

Justin Allen: Yeah. And that's how you could say it's an amazing thing or it's a sublime thing. Or you give a descriptive word that seems impressive because in a sense it is, if your whole life everything's about recognizing, and then all of a sudden there's no recognition happening, it's a shock, it's like, wow, look...

Andreas Müller: Yes. That's a funny thing. It actually, it should be a shock, but there is something so amazing and attractive about it that, it's amazing. (laughing)

Justin Allen: Yeah. But it is in a way to just to go to a refrigerator and open up the door without you being there to do it, it is an amazing thing. Even if you take away comparing. It's amazing because you're comparing it to how you were always there opening up the refrigerator, but even without the idea of comparison, that everything's just happening without anything there to make it happen.

Andreas Müller: Yeah. Yeah. There isn't anyone really conscious about it.

Justin Allen: That's it (laughing).

Andreas Müller: All right (laughing). Cool. That's it.

Justin Allen: Yeah.

Andreas Müller: So there's nothing to recognize. There is no recognition already.

Andreas Müller: All right.

Justin Allen: Yeah.

Andreas Müller: Okay. Lovely to see you.

Justin Allen: Happy to see you too.

Andreas Müller: Yeah. And thank you very much everyone for watching and joining. Have a lovely day, evening. Bye. Thank you. Bye.

Justin Allen: Bye.

EVEN THE MICROSCOPE CONFIRMS YOU'RE NOT THERE

Andreas Müller:	Yeah. It works (laughing)! All right. How are you doing?
Justin Allen:	Good. How are you?
Andreas Müller:	I'm fine.
Justin Allen:	You look like you got a fresh haircut or something.
Andreas Müller:	Yeah, actually, it is fresher (laughing).
Justin Allen:	Okay. (silence)
Andreas Müller:	I'm ready.
Justin Allen:	You're not going to do the same introduction thing?
Andreas Müller:	Ah, I wasn't sure, did I do something like an introduction?
Justin Allen:	All the other times you did.
Andreas Müller:	Ah, all right. Okay. So, again, welcome everyone to the conversation between Justin and me. So I don't really know what this will be about today. I guess, it will have something to do with non-duality (laughing).
Justin Allen:	Maybe (laughing).

Andreas Müller: Maybe, yeah. So feel free (to begin). We said that it's just a conversation between us, so ...

Justin Allen: That's it?

Andreas Müller: That's it. Yeah.

Justin Allen: All right. What I'm curious about is, do you remember what we talked about last time?

Andreas Müller: Not right now (laughing), but I think I'll remember when you just mention it again.

Justin Allen: I don't remember either.

Andreas Müller: Ah, okay. Okay. So, no, I have no idea.

Justin Allen: Do you remember any of the conversations we had (laughing)?

Andreas Müller: No, not really (laughing).

Justin Allen: Do you remember liking one more than the other?

Andreas Müller: Yeah. I think I remember something. We talked about this sentence "I don't know."

Justin Allen: Yeah. That was one where there was a dominant theme.

Andreas Müller: Yeah, exactly. I remember that one a bit, yeah.

Justin Allen: So one thing I wanted to ask, I thought about it on the way to this meeting, was how, without, let's say, without the searching energy of other people, you don't have ... you wouldn't have a platform really, or you wouldn't have (laughing) anything to say (laughing).

Andreas Müller: I mean, yes (laughing). This meeting, this message, depends on the people being seekers, yes.

Justin Allen: Yeah.

Andreas Müller: Oh, totally (laughing).

Justin Allen: I was thinking about that on the way to this meeting. I was thinking about, for example, if I have nothing to say (laughing) or nothing to contribute, then you also can't really generate that much to talk about.

Andreas Müller: Oh, and not at all.

Justin Allen: Yeah. Well, some of it, you can, in the sense, like you (can give a basic introduction) ... Do you know what I mean?

Andreas Müller: I just thought that's the hidden reason for why (laughing) there is no method.

Justin Allen: Yeah (laughing).

Andreas Müller: I don't want anyone's "me" to drop (laughing). I need you all.

Justin Allen: Yeah, exactly. (laughing)

Andreas Müller: No, no. I don't, of course.

Justin Allen: But I was thinking about how when you give, one of your formal talks, then, generally, you talk for, maximum, five minutes, where you just say this is about nothing and "no one" and then that triggers, that triggers the searching energy from other people or that provokes them with questions. Not that that's what you're doing. I'm just saying that's the nature of the searching energy. So without that, though, you can't really give out information or you can't really do anything.

Andreas Müller: Yes, and even the introduction is ... Actually, one could, not that there is someone doing it, but, in a way, that's the most difficult part, the introduction, to just say something out of nothing. That's impossible, actually.

Justin Allen: Yeah. So, for you, using you as a case study that is seemingly different than everybody else's situation, when you come to your talk, you really have nothing to talk about.

Andreas Müller: Yes.

Justin Allen: And you're there, like a blank slate, and then from your "no-point perspective," you're just ... whatever's coming out is what's coming out, almost. Not like you're doing it, almost like there's something typing sentences for you to talk about.

Andreas Müller: Yes, yeah. There's absolutely ... and that's honest. I really mean it like that. There's absolutely nothing that I want to say.

Justin Allen: Right.

Andreas Müller: It's not like me...

Justin Allen: You're not saying it. It's just being said and it seems like it's being said by you.

Andreas Müller: Yes, exactly, but it's not that I appear in front of an audience having something in mind saying, "Oh, that's what I really want to say today. That's what they need to hear," or something.

Justin Allen: Right.

Andreas Müller: No, it's really blank. I've honestly nothing to say.

Justin Allen: So when you do start off your talk and you start talking, then it's really just spontaneous. It's not pre-planned or contrived or ...

Andreas Müller: No.

Justin Allen: ... but it could also happen that, on the way to your talk or 10 minutes before your talk or 30 minutes before your talk, it could happen that maybe a theme arises that maybe you then say, "Ah, that might be interesting to start my talk off with..."

Andreas Müller: This might happen, but to be honest, when the meeting starts, it's hardly (laughing) those sentences that came up half an hour before.

Justin Allen: Yeah.

Andreas Müller: So there wouldn't really be a connection, but it might actually be what happens.

Justin Allen: But even if there were a connection, let's say, a day before, let's just say that a day before your talk, something happened and it triggered a thought where you said, "Maybe this would be interesting to talk about."

Andreas Müller: No, that's too far away because, actually, I'm also, it's hard to describe, but I'm actually also blank about even having a next talk. So this is not something that I now already think about that, "Oh, tomorrow I have a talk where I have to say something." It might be there. The idea that I'll have a talk tomorrow might be there on a functional level because I have a calendar and stuff, but there's absolutely no idea about the content of it.

Justin Allen: Yeah.

Andreas Müller: Yeah.

Justin Allen: So then, for you, in that sense, and even for us listening, it really is just spontaneously coming out, and then it is like you are not doing the ... you're not even talking, the talking's just happening...

Andreas Müller:	And my impression is, actually, the energy of this meeting, this message, is rather an answering. It's not offering anything or it's not putting out information because it's so interesting. It's rather an apparent answering to the seeking energy, and in a way...
Justin Allen:	Which you start off talking about, though, even before somebody asks a question.
Andreas Müller:	Yeah, but, in a way, that's what I wanted to say, in a way the energy is already there (implying the seeking energy from apparent "people" and responding to that energy).
Justin Allen:	That's what I wanted to say.
Andreas Müller:	Yeah.
Justin Allen:	That's what I meant by without that energy that's already out there and existing, you have nothing, you would really have nothing to ... (say)
Andreas Müller:	Yeah.
Justin Allen:	Because when you start off talking, somebody hasn't asked a question yet, and if you already say, "There's nobody there. This non-duality is about nobody's there. Things are just happening. There's just this." You're responding to a fact or general knowledge that there's a bunch of searching energy out there. People thinking that they are there and it's in response to that.
Andreas Müller:	One could say so, yes, it's already in the air.
Justin Allen:	Yeah.
Andreas Müller:	That may be an apparent story. I mean, part of it certainly is just out of convention. There is an

apparent meeting set up and you say hello and blah, blah, blah, but, in the end, the seeking energy is already there without there having been asked a question.

Justin Allen: Yeah, yeah.

Andreas Müller: That's my impression. That's why it doesn't really work to say this provokes the seeking.

Justin Allen: Right. Yeah, true. That doesn't make sense that it ...

Andreas Müller: No. It puts the focus on this issue maybe. What it does, it puts the focus on, the attention on what we speak about here, so to say.

Justin Allen: Yeah, because there's a different ... There is, let's say that any other, what we, in this context, what we would call a teacher, and it doesn't have to be a spiritual teacher. It could be a teacher of how to make money. Let's use that as an alternative. They're also provoking. A teacher of how to make money is provoking you. She's provoking an audience that doesn't have money and wants it, let's say, or that wants more of it.

Andreas Müller: Yeah.

Justin Allen: So then that teacher would be putting out this information in a way to provoke and then also would get questions from an audience of how to get money (the audience also provokes the money-making teacher)?

Andreas Müller: Yes.

Justin Allen: And then a spiritual teacher provokes, in the sense, like pointing out also that you're not fully realized, let's say, that you haven't discovered your true self yet, and then, as an audience, then they say, "Yeah, I want to find my true self." So then comes a series of questions.

Andreas Müller: Yes.

Justin Allen: And then, in this case, you are not provoking by saying that this is how you need to change or this is what needs to happen or offering something, but you're answering to an energy that has nothing to do with a person or it's not personal or it has nothing to do with individuals saying, just pointing out that this energy of searching and thinking that you're there, that there's somebody there, isn't the case.

Andreas Müller: Yes. Yeah, it's not even pointing that out to anyone. It's just that it can't be explained really because it's just what seems to be happening, but it's just a direct response. Not even to point it out to anyone.

Justin Allen: Yeah. Pointing it out is the wrong word, also, because then it implies that you are there doing it, but ...

Andreas Müller: And as if there were a goal, but it's just, "Hey, there isn't anyone," but not in order to convince anyone or to point that out, to make it clear to the others, so to speak. It's just a, "Oh, there isn't anyone."

Justin Allen: So when you start off talking and you say that there isn't anyone, then this is just repeating. Then you're just answering out of nothing.

Andreas Müller: Kind of, yeah (laughing). I mean, you can't really know how it actually is. What's really going on, you can't know, but, yes, that's what seems to be happening, yeah, because it's just happening that I'm offering those talks, so to speak.

Justin Allen: Yeah.

Andreas Müller: That somehow ... but it doesn't come out of a need or a plan or that I think I need to do that or ... "I'm a teacher." Then there would be a teacher. There would be someone having a clear goal in mind who would know what this is about, would experience him or herself to be someone, and then there would be all those ingredients. There's a goal, I have to tell you something. It's important what I have to say, and stuff like that.

Justin Allen: And when you say that, then, I can't help but acknowledge that there is a confusion in that, and the confusion, I'll point it out, is that what you just said from your case that it's just an answering to an energetic question that's out there, but you're not really answering it. It's just then, in your case, it's also just ... an energetic output.

Andreas Müller: Yeah, yeah. If you want, so ... yes.

Justin Allen: But then you're not there really answering any of these questions and you're not there when you talk. You're not there giving a talk and you're not there making a point, but then, at the same time, all the people that are in the audience with the searching energy, that are looking for something and wanting something, so it seems like they're there with a purpose, right? And it seems like they're there with an intention and a goal. I mean, the opposite of what you just said.

Andreas Müller: Yeah (laughing). So to speak, yes.

Justin Allen: From your case.

Andreas Müller: Yeah.

Justin Allen:
But they also don't really have a goal (Andreas confirms) and they also ... Yeah, so that's what I wanted to say, that's the thing, it's confusing in the sense that... Let's say that I took your words verbatim without being able to, potentially, read between the lines or to just, resonate with what you are saying or somehow understand it without understanding. Somehow, paradoxically, I know what you mean, let's say.

Justin Allen:
If I don't know what you mean, then when I hear you saying that there's "no one" there and you're just energetically answering to the world or to an energy, but you're saying it in the sense that a teacher, if we compare yourself to a teacher, they wouldn't be giving a talk and answering questions the way that you are because the way that you are responding, is you're not doing it with intention and they are doing it with intention.

Andreas Müller:
Absolutely.

Justin Allen:
But in reality, in the context of your talks, they're (the teachers) also not really doing it with an intention.

Andreas Müller:
Yes. One could say so. They are not ... or this whole thing would happen equally intention-less.

Justin Allen:
Right.

Andreas Müller:
It would just be what apparently happens without any real intention.

Justin Allen:
Yeah.

Andreas Müller:
Yeah. Totally, yes.

Justin Allen:
So let's say that you and I are talking about a teacher and we're ... It seems almost like we're

critical of a teacher or that we're laughing about how a teacher thinks that they know and thinks that they're there giving the talk, right (laughing)?

Andreas Müller: Yeah (laughing).

Justin Allen: But it also has no quality behind it or no substance behind it because that teacher really isn't there teaching, and that teacher also isn't really there with an intention.

Andreas Müller: Absolutely. Though, she would claim something else (laughing). She would claim to be there, and she would even claim to have an intention to help the world or save the poor seekers, but, yes, it would be totally illusory. It would just be dreamt within her story. Within the total story. So it's not happening. Me teaching, intention, all this personal stuff, isn't really happening.

Justin Allen: And, in a sense, that would just be that energetic "whatever," if we're going to call it energy, then that teacher would have an energetic ... That teacher isn't actually teaching. It's just what's coming out of (her) ... it's just the words that are coming out of them that form this network of what we would call teaching.

Andreas Müller: Yeah, but including the illusion that there is someone.

Justin Allen: Right, but that's still part ... that would also be an energetic (apparent happening) ...

Andreas Müller: Yes.

Justin Allen: Right. That's what I mean.

Andreas Müller: Yeah.

Justin Allen:	Let's say you're not actually talking and you're not actually in control of what you say. It's just what's coming out.
Andreas Müller:	Yes.
Justin Allen:	The teacher also isn't in control of what he or she is teaching or what her or his intention is, but on top of that energy of them (apparently) teaching, there's also the energy of them (apparently) sensing that they're there (apparently) teaching.
Andreas Müller:	Exactly. Yes.
Justin Allen:	So let's say that you're on a basic level of energy where you just ... things (laughing) ... You're on a parasitic level (laughing) of energetic output, let's say, and then a teacher has another level of it where they think that they're there.
Andreas Müller:	That's what seems to be happening, yeah.
Justin Allen:	Yeah. So there's no, again ... I mean, we've talked about this before, but then that levels the playing field, in a sense too, where it dilutes everything to just being all the same again and there not being any real differences.
Andreas Müller:	Yes, exactly. This message doesn't recognize differences. It doesn't recognize...
Justin Allen:	Superficially, it does.
Andreas Müller:	Well, yeah. Apparently, it can point out apparent differences. That's incomprehensible. What does that mean? Apparent differences. Is it different or not? No, it's apparently different, but it doesn't regard this as real differences.
Justin Allen:	But from hearing this and from one point of view,

I could say, "Okay, there is a difference between Andreas. He is not teaching and he is not telling me what to do and he's not ..." There's no intention.

Andreas Müller: Oh, which, of course, is a contradiction in itself already. Andreas is not teaching. (It is a contradiction because there is no Andreas to be teaching or not teaching.)

Justin Allen: Yeah. All right.

Andreas Müller: You know what I mean?

Justin Allen: Yeah. Well, let's say Andreas is blank (laughing), and whatever output isn't actually output from somebody behind the scenes, it's just output. Output without any past, output without any source, basically.

Andreas Müller: Yeah, yeah. Output without any person. It's not personal.

Justin Allen: ... with a teacher, in any traditional sense or conventional sense, with a teacher, there's also, in fact, not any source, not any person.

Andreas Müller: Yes.

Justin Allen: But then the (apparent) difference is, is that there's the belief that there is, or the sense that there is someone there.

Andreas Müller: Exactly. That would be an apparent difference.

Justin Allen: And one thing I wanted to say right now that I wanted to just interject, if that teacher was teaching and thought that whatever was coming out was from them or from some source that they were identifying with in some way, and then that energetic sense of being there disappeared, that person, from your point of view, could no longer teach.

Andreas Müller: Yes. I would say so, yeah.

Justin Allen: So that's where it seems like there's another difference, and I just want to continue because, if we were saying that everybody is the same in the sense that nobody is actually there, and then there's an energetic... While someone is here (when there is this sense of someone), there's an energetic push or pull to teach (or be taught), and so I go teaching and telling everybody how to be and believing that I've found the right way to be. Then, if that disappeared, because it wasn't really happening in the first place, why wouldn't I just continue teaching?

Andreas Müller: Because what we talk about (laughing) is, on the one hand, utterly ordinary, on the other hand, it's not logical at all (laughing). It doesn't make sense, but, as I say, it's much, much more ordinary. So when there's the illusion to be someone and there is seeking and teaching, I mean, teaching is actually seeking too. It comes out of a seeking energy, basically, the teaching, and when that isn't anymore, then teaching isn't possible anymore.

Andreas Müller: I know, and at first it may not ... It's not what we talk about. It isn't really black and white in that sense, but this whole setup just collapses. It doesn't mean that, overnight, those sentences couldn't be spoken. I mean, I know a lot of therapists and healers and stuff, and, of course, when the "me" drops or when this illusion to be someone drops, they might go on with their job or doing what they do, but suddenly it would just change because it's impossible for them to really see someone who needs to be taught. But it's not that, overnight, maybe you have the so-called teacher or therapist that would quit everything. Somehow, this would follow organically, so to speak.

Justin Allen: Yeah.

Andreas Müller: It might also be possible that they quit overnight, and next morning come up, "Hey, guys. Sorry, there's nothing to do (laughing)."

Justin Allen: And just to paint a picture and follow this pattern or this path a little bit further, imagine that I'm a therapist and I've been for 20 years "helping" people work out their problems, and I believe, somehow ... I don't think most therapists think that they've figured it all out, generally. Let's assume that most therapists don't think that they are living the best life or they know everything.

Andreas Müller: Yeah. I mean, therapists nowadays are quite cool, actually. They already got quite humble (laughing).

Justin Allen: Yeah. Like a spiritual teacher, let's say a conventional, modern, current spiritual teacher, they act and seem like they know how to live life the right way and they've figured it all out.

Andreas Müller: Absolutely, and that's also the picture they present.

Justin Allen: Right. So let's just use the therapist where a therapist doesn't really ... they don't hold their selves to be such high-esteemers or so developed, let's say, but they're there still trying to help people out to manage their lives.

Andreas Müller: It's just another concept.

Justin Allen: Right.

Andreas Müller: It may be a bit more ordinary than the spiritual teacher who sits on a throne and stuff, but, I mean, there aren't so many of them also. There are a lot of spiritual teachers who run their small groups and where they are also rather ordinary, but, yeah, the mindset is a different one, the story. It's more like friendship and we know each other. Yeah, I think it's, nowadays, much more about this personal connection therapy, like to meet the patients as a human being and stuff like that.

Justin Allen: But still, as a therapist, they think that they're ... they would imagine that they might be improving the lives of one of their patients.

Andreas Müller: Of course, it's still a position. Even they play, it's not meant in a bad way, but even though they play in a more friendly (way), not really hierarchical and more to be aware, just listen, giving space for the patient, it's still a position that's made by someone, and it's still personal, of course. They still believe in a dynamic, which is supportive for the person.

Justin Allen: Exactly, and so imagine that that therapist that's been believing that or feeling that for 20 years, and then, all of a sudden, they're not there anymore, but this is their livelihood and this is their routine and how they've been going through life for 20 years. You don't know, you can't, of course, you can't say, "How's this person then going to continue on with life," but let's just say that, this one case, they say, "Okay, I'm not giving up being a therapist," and they continue to do therapy, and based on what you said previously, within this context, then that person might still continue to "help" people manage their lives, but it might just be subtly different. The energy that they're ... or their output ... (might change or would in fact change, apparently)

Andreas Müller: Absolutely.

Justin Allen:	... to the patient, and then the way that they acknowledge this patient would no longer be ...
Andreas Müller:	Personal.
Justin Allen:	... seeing this person as a person that has to go through life in certain ways.
Andreas Müller:	Absolutely. Absolutely, and (it's a story, and, yes, no one knows) my impression is that it would quite organically move more and more into what's happening here (referring to these no-point perspective talks / non-duality talks / no-thing message).
Justin Allen:	And then let's say that if it moved (laughing) more organically to what's happening here (laughing), and then I go to the therapist and I start going through all my problems and asking for help, the therapist might start to run out of therapy options or things to (advise me on or methods to work on) ... It might start to become more of a no treatment, in a sense, because that's what I was ... That's why, when I started off talking about this, you need that searching energy, in a way, to have a conversation about non-duality.
Andreas Müller:	Or that I need interest. It's not actually the ... It's both because the seeking energy is there, the moment there is the sense of a person, but it's actually the seeking energy and an apparent resonance with this message.
Justin Allen:	Yeah, but if all the people here that came to your talks were just asking for life advice, which generally doesn't happen ... not that I have so much experience, but if you go to spiritual teachers, it seems like, of the two times that I've been, that a lot of the questions, the majority of the questions, are really, really personal.

Andreas Müller: Yeah.

Justin Allen: Whereas here it stays on topic, and I think the reason why it stays on topic, in a way, is because those questions don't have any energy anymore (or much less energy).

Andreas Müller: Absolutely.

Justin Allen: Right.

Andreas Müller: That's also what the introduction is for (laughing).

Justin Allen: Right, to weed out the (spirit, hope, idolatry) (laughing) ... but as a therapist, I feel like it would be trying. Therapy would become a much more difficult job in this context.

Andreas Müller: Yeah, it's possible. Yep.

Justin Allen: So then, yeah, you don't know. I'm just playing out a scenario.

Andreas Müller: Yeah.

Justin Allen: So then another scenario would be is that, you were interested in spirituality, for lack of a better word, and you pursued this intensely for 20 years or something, or 15 years (laughing), and then, for you, the "me" fell away, but then you continued. Not that it's this ... you're not in the same (field), but you're more or less in the same category. It's not like you became a bus driver or you became an architect or you became a scientist. You stayed in the same field. (Spirituality to non-spirituality)

Andreas Müller: Yeah. One could ... Yeah, almost. Yeah, yep.

Justin Allen: And so that's what I was thinking about how, of the non-duality people, in a way, that I'm most familiar with would be you, Jim Newman and, I guess, Tony Parsons, and all three of you had a similar interest (and origin). You, and it seems like Jim Newman, seem to be more into spirituality than Tony Parsons, but I don't really know his background as well. Then you stay in this field, and it seems natural in a way.

Andreas Müller: Yeah. I don't know, because in my story, it was actually … Well, when I met Tony, for example, and I met this message, for me it really felt as if I've completely left spirituality, for example.

Justin Allen: Right.

Andreas Müller: That's how it really felt, and when the "me" dropped, it actually felt as if I'm leaving non-duality now as well, because non-duality dropped too, and it was really rather surprising and amazing that the talks started because it was really, when the "me" dropped or when I died, there was absolutely nothing left, and there was also no sense of to just go on in this surrounding or stuff like that. In that sense, it was just a miracle in the end.

Justin Allen: But just to compare, let's just say that instead of you having spent your formative years and then your early 20s in spirituality and living a lifestyle that allowed you to pursue spirituality intensely, and instead of doing that, you were a scientist that studied cancer or something. So then you turned 40 years old and your life has been studying cancer, it's your whole world, and then, all of a sudden, the "me" drops and then you're there in this (lab) … your friends are all scientists, and your whole life revolves around science, and then how are you going to start giving (laughing) talks (about non-duality called the Timeless Wonder) …

Andreas Müller: Yeah (laughing). It's impossible, but, yeah, it sounds a bit theoretical, but I know what you mean.

Justin Allen:

All I mean from that is that this is going back to, in a way, like you just said, "You are not there," but there's a character there and there's a conditioning that's there, right? And that character that's there is, let's say, genetic, and then how you were raised and all this stuff. Not that it's you that was raised a certain way, but this thing that's you, you're different than other people, character wise and physically and everything.

Andreas Müller:

Yeah. All right.

Justin Allen:

So, superficially, there's real differences between you and me.

Andreas Müller:

Yeah. I understand. In the story, so to speak. Totally.

Justin Allen:

Right. So, in a sense, you're limited, of course ...

Andreas Müller:

Of course.

Justin Allen:

... you're never going to be an NBA basketball player and, of course, in your case, you're not going to develop a cure for cancer or anything like that. So, in a way, even though, for you, the "me" dropped, but you're still ... for you, maybe you continue on giving talks and this is your way because that's how your character already was/is.

Andreas Müller:

Absolutely. Oh, I know what you mean. Yes.

Justin Allen:

So that's what I just wanted to say, is the people that you generally hear, that you listen to talk about non-duality, also seem to be people that were pursuing it (the majority of the speakers at least in 2021), somehow, not necessarily pursuing non-duality, but pursuing a spiritual path.

Andreas Müller:

I always say, the number is so small that I think it's not representative.

Justin Allen:	Yeah. I just wanted to say, but if there were more people, you wouldn't even know about them because why would they ...
Andreas Müller:	Oh, yeah. I mean, there are more people speaking about it. I wouldn't be surprised if there would be people without any background giving seminars, in a broader sense even, or holding seminars or speaking about energy. It wouldn't...
Justin Allen:	Right. It might be an entrepreneur developing new products for the aluminum siding market and having a family and a normal life that you'll never hear talk about this.
Andreas Müller:	It's possible, but I wouldn't be surprised if someone with that background would also start to talk about this. It wouldn't surprise me.
Justin Allen:	And to set up a talk where they host events every week?
Andreas Müller:	Absolutely, yeah.
Justin Allen:	And that, from your perspective, the reason why that might be possible is because, for them, also, might arise this answering, an answering to a searching energy.
Andreas Müller:	Yeah, because it would just be what apparently happens, and I know, it seems much more logical and ordinary with me having that background and coming from that background, but, in the end, within my story, this was as illogical as everything else.
Justin Allen:	Yeah.
Andreas Müller:	I know what you mean. It looks as if it fits, and apparently it does, but to me it wasn't logical at all. I really didn't know why should I start the meetings

at all. I mean, at first I thought, "Why should I give meetings"? I mean, they can see Tony. It was utterly useless me doing them, even in the story, I thought, "It's, well, come on (laughing). As long as Tony's doing talks, why would I ..." So it was really illogical.

Andreas Müller: I mean, for the first years, I had totally different plans. I was giving the talks, but in the first years I thought I'd go on as a driver, and my former boss had plans for me where he wanted to have a bigger business. I could go into this business with him. That was actually my plan. I didn't see this going on like it has. I thought it just remains like I started in Germany, have a weekend here and there and stuff. I mean, it's still possible again, but, as I said, when it started, it was not that this was the logical conclusion from my path. It wasn't even the logical conclusion from the dropping of the "me," because, in a way, if you take this concept, the logical conclusion would exactly be to not start talks.

Justin Allen: Yeah. Well, then again, just because I like to come back to this point where nothing makes sense again (laughing). It's like, for you, you have no control. That you're giving these talks is just out of control. There's no reason why it's happening. It's just that's what's happening, and you can look back and you can try to find a pattern or try to find a logical reason, but there's not one.

Andreas Müller: Absolutely.

Justin Allen: And then same with a spiritual teacher. There is no control why they're there standing up saying, "I have figured it out and you guys need to do this and this and this."

Andreas Müller: Yeah. They are not doing it either (laughing).

Justin Allen: Exactly.

Andreas Müller: That's the wildness of wholeness. It can even appear as a spiritual teacher claiming, "I am God. Pray to me."

Justin Allen: So, just as equally as you have no control of what you say and what you're apparently doing, these spiritual teachers and therapists also have no control.

Andreas Müller: Yes. Not at all. Not a single bit. That's why it's okay to make fun of them (laughing). There isn't anyone anyway who could be hurt or stuff like that. There is no one.

Justin Allen: But, and then again, to make it equally as confusing, if this spiritual teacher, then energetically lost the sense of self, they would no longer be spiritually teaching (although they may apparently go on "teaching").

Andreas Müller: Yes, exactly. Which, as we said in the beginning, theoretically, why shouldn't he go on being a spiritual seeker of the world, but ... True, but actually I don't see how this is possible.

Justin Allen: So then they might, for them, the most that they could do, or the most similar way that they might continue, because it could be a career, the spiritual teaching might be a career, and then if they changed, then their change might be, let's say, from one day ... yesterday they were saying, "You guys need to do this, and do this and this. You need to realize this and this," and then the next day they lose their energy and they, one week later, they have organized a talk, they might come up on stage then and say, "You guys, you're not there." (laughing)

Andreas Müller:	It might also be more organic, but, yeah, of course, it wouldn't be possible (to teach). Not because now he or she has something else to say.
Justin Allen:	Right. It's just that they can't help it anymore, just like they couldn't help it before.
Andreas Müller:	Exactly, and there would be no energy anymore to keep that other stuff up, to keep that crap up while they are trying to teach someone. It would be impossible and empty, and it would feel like a lie, even if they would be trying at first, so to speak, or there would be a trying at first to keep that role up, but it would collapse, over time, at least. It's a story. That's what I believe, so to say, but I don't know how this would be able to be kept up. It's impossible because no role can be kept up as a role when there is "no one" anymore.
Justin Allen:	So that would be … You can put that into the context of a person that's there. A person that's there could understand that from a personal perspective quite easily.
Andreas Müller:	What do you mean?
Justin Allen:	I mean, Hollywood's grabbed onto that concept, the concept of where the actor is living a lie and then they can't do it anymore and then they … whatever … but your parents said that you need to be a doctor, so then the person works hard to become a doctor, even though it's not what they really want to do. Then, at some point, they realize that they're living a lie and then they stop being a doctor.
Andreas Müller:	Yeah, but, usually, in Hollywood, then they start to live their truth (laughing).
Justin Allen:	Right. They live their truth as a baker.

Andreas Müller: Exactly (laughing).

Justin Allen: So that's what I mean, within the personal energetic context, that's how they would hear this, in a way. That's how they could relate to this message.

Andreas Müller: Yeah, and, in a way, it's not even too different. That's what I mean, what we speak about...

Justin Allen: It's not too different, but the big difference is just that you're not there ever and there's "no one" there that's the baker anymore. They think that they realize something, and they say, "I was living a lie and now I'm going to live the truth."

Andreas Müller: Exactly. I mean, what we talk about here is very ordinary, in a way. It's not special or superhuman or stuff like that. It's very ordinary. No, it's all...

Justin Allen: That's ordinary too. It's ordinary to have an energy that takes you in one direction, and then to have a, not that it's a different energy, but that you go in a different direction.

Andreas Müller: Yeah.

Justin Allen: The only difference is, is that, for you, in your case, you don't take claim for any direction that you go, but then the majority of cases there's a claiming of (a direction or of a "doership") ...

Andreas Müller: I mean, with the lie, it would immediately be replaced with another truth, seriously. Yep, and apparently that doesn't seem to happen here. It's just the fading out of any personal story or role or stuff like that.

Justin Allen: And that's why, I think we've said this, or I've said this in every one of our talks almost, you come back to this whole ... you always come back to the same thing, but that's why it would be said, how you say, in a sense, the realization or the awakening or the shift or the dropping away or the melting away of the "me," is that the recognition or the realization that there never was a "me" and there never ... and the way that works contextually, the way that we're talking about it now, is just that there was only, in a sense, this energy without anything behind it.

Andreas Müller: Yes.

Justin Allen: So whether it presents itself going in this direction, then switching to this direction, each time there was actually never anyone behind it, even when you thought that there was.

Andreas Müller: Yes, exactly. Totally. Never (laughing). It was all ... it's all wholeness, so to speak, all the time.

Justin Allen: That's when you say, because that's all that there is, that's all that there can be (Andreas confirms). There's just ... but I'm just paraphrasing, or actually verbatim saying what you say, that's where it comes from, kind of.

Andreas Müller: Yep, and that's, again, when there is no difference, there isn't a real difference recognized between anything.

Justin Allen: Yeah. There can't be a difference recognized between inanimate objects and animate objects. In the sense, like you say, the wall is walling, right? You give an action to something that, generally, we would call actionless.

Andreas Müller: Yeah.

Justin Allen: You give the wall a quality of action, but what you're describing is that the same way you're like a wall, or as a human, you're just humaning, and what humans tend to do is move around and talk and ...

Andreas Müller: Exactly, yeah.

Justin Allen: What walls tend to do is stay still and divide.

Andreas Müller: Yeah, exactly. I'm a human wall.

Justin Allen: Yeah, and we generally accept all that with everything except ourselves, in a way. Generally, we don't think that birds are there, and we...

Andreas Müller: And that birds could become or something.

Justin Allen: We think birds are more there, than a wall, but, in a sense, we don't think that a bird is there or that an insect is there, and we definitely don't think that a wall is there.

Andreas Müller: Yeah, or that they can be anything else than what they are.

Justin Allen: Right. Yeah, a wall can't become a better wall (laughing).

Andreas Müller: Yeah, exactly.

Justin Allen: The wall can't. We can make the wall "better" (laughing).

Andreas Müller: Yeah, I was just about to say, the wall can't become a better wall out of itself (laughing), but the moment there is self-consciousness, there is the idea, "Oh, but I can make it better," again.

Justin Allen: And we also don't really think a bird can make itself a better bird. Generally, we don't think that birds are training somehow to become better birds. We look at birds and we might judge them and say, "That one's better than that one, but ..."

Andreas Müller: They don't even recognize that.

Justin Allen:	Right, and we accept that, but we don't accept it with ourselves, even though it's the exact same case. Just like a bird flying is just … We think the bird's flying there and, at most, at best, scientifically, we just say that they're doing it out of Darwinism, evolutionary reasons, but, really, you look outside and you accept the trees just … It's not doing whatever it does with intention. It's just pre-programmed, basically, and …
Andreas Müller:	So to speak, yeah.
Justin Allen:	… circumstantially. If you plant a tree without any trees around, it doesn't have to compete, so it can become a full, big tree.
Andreas Müller:	Except some spiritual people. Spiritual people would be able to imply intention even in trees and even in stones, as if everything has its place and plays a purpose in the big existence and stuff. So it is possible for the "I am" to even invent purpose to things and stuff, but yeah, generally, I know what you mean.
Justin Allen:	But the same way that, as a general person, that you don't think that a wall can make itself into a better wall or improve itself somehow, because all it can do is that (wall). All it can be is just the wall, and then, really, that's all that you are also, is that you're just … there's nothing there that can improve itself or do anything actively. You're not there doing anything. Life is just (apparently) doing things through (an apparent) you. The same way that the wall … the only way that the wall is going to change is if we change it, basically, or a force changes it.
Andreas Müller:	Yep. In that sense, I am the same, or everything or everyone is the same like everything else. Totally, already, all the time.

Justin Allen:	And that's something that I wanted to add, if you were fading away (or when you were "fading" away), did you ever feel like you were having a ... trying to avoid the word glimpse? Did you ever start to feel or sense that nothing's different? (as in a glimpse)
Andreas Müller:	Yeah. That's always hard to say. In a way, yes. Well, that's where you can't really go with words anymore. It just became more and more obvious, meaning it just was more and more like that.
Justin Allen:	Yeah.
Andreas Müller:	It wasn't really me becoming aware of how nothing is different from each other. Suddenly nothing, while it happened, so to speak, there was nothing claiming anymore, "Oh, this is different. Oh, this was that."
Justin Allen:	And then, that sense ... maybe there was some weaker sense of that, and then it strengthened and then, at some point, it just was insignificant.
Andreas Müller:	Yeah.
Justin Allen:	And that, if you use the word amazing or if you use a word similar to amazing, that's what you're describing, because it's so contrary to how you ... If you're really seeing yourself as something there that can (seemingly) control itself and make things better or worse and that can act and that is responsible, and then you look out and you see everything as being totally different and separate and hierarchies and qualities, and then that starts to dilute, and then it dilutes completely to where you really can't, outside of superficially, you really can't just make a distinction anymore.
Andreas Müller:	Yeah.

| Justin Allen: | Because, before if you hear a noise, it's definitely you're hearing a noise outside of you, but then if the context or if the point isn't there anymore, then it just all blends in with everything. (ordinary) |

Andreas Müller: Yes. Automatic, ordinarily. When this illusion of the "I" drops, what's being described here, apparently, is the only and natural reality. It just is like that, but I can't describe or know what this means or how this exactly is. It just ...

Justin Allen: It would be like ... No, it wouldn't be like that. I was going to try to make an analogy (laughing), but it would be, like you've heard ... The only one that comes to mind is how in spirituality, poetic spirituality, they talk about how you identify yourself being a wave (in the ocean), the wave isn't really different than the ocean. Or how do you isolate a drop of beer in a beer glass as separate from the beer?

Andreas Müller: Oh, what do you mean?

Justin Allen: I mean, you can't really distinguish ... you can't make any distinction from a drop inside of the beer or ... (a drop of ocean from the ocean)

Andreas Müller: From the beer. Yes, exactly.

Justin Allen: ... a drop inside of the ocean, or if you could zoom out right now, way out into the galaxy or something like that, and you realize when you go far enough away in the galaxy that all it is, is a bunch of (space)... I don't know ... or the same way if you look at your skin with a magnifying glass or a microscope, and you see that your skin is just made up of a bunch of things moving around. It might not even be that it's solid, or when scientists look at things they're describing, nothing's actually solid. All it is, is particles (bacteria, viruses, microorganisms, cells, atoms, etc.) that are moving at different speeds and the different speeds create the density. (Which we call solid or less solid)

Andreas Müller: Yeah. I mean, the way ... Yeah, but it would be like that, but not for anyone that's...

Justin Allen: Right, but, I mean, you can't help it, of course, but if you were able to look ... If you looked at your skin and all of a sudden you started to see it as really being made up of Zillions of moving "things," and the first layer might be bacteria and then the second layer, the bacteria isn't even bacteria, that's just made up of other little things, that you can't help but feel like you're still there because that's an energetic thing, but, in reality, it's like you can't be there, because the wall is also made up of the same moving things.

Andreas Müller: Yes. Yeah, absolutely.

Justin Allen: So you would vanish ...

Andreas Müller: Exactly.

Justin Allen: The way that you vanished, it just happened, in a way, but it would almost, you could almost make people vanish if you could show how ... You know what I mean, though? If you could show that you're not really there, and the only way that you could show that you're not really there would be a huge people-looking-microscope.

Andreas Müller: Yeah. I know what you mean, but...

Justin Allen: Even that wouldn't work because, as you're saying, it's an energetic thing, but you know what I mean.

Andreas Müller: Exactly.

Justin Allen:	I mean, that's the most amazing thing, actually, is that even if you could scientifically or with a microscope show (physically and theoretically prove) that you're not there ... (laughing)
Andreas Müller:	You would still feel to be there (laughing). Exactly, which would give you the constant feeling of, "Well, actually I do know, but ..."
Justin Allen:	Yeah.
Andreas Müller:	Which many spiritual seekers have, actually. Well, "I know that there is 'no one,' but I'm still seeking ...."
Justin Allen:	That's true.
Andreas Müller:	Yeah.
Justin Allen:	All right. Maybe we should wrap it up.
Andreas Müller:	All right.
Justin Allen:	When is ... We have another one again in August.
Andreas Müller:	We have another one already in August. I think it's in a month. It's the 15th of August.
Justin Allen:	So, August 15th.
Andreas Müller:	Yeah, exactly.
Justin Allen:	Okay.
Andreas Müller:	Yeah. All right.
Justin Allen:	All right.
Andreas Müller:	Cool. Okay, all right, everyone. Thanks for joining. Have a nice time. Thank you very much, Justin.

Justin Allen: Thank you. Bye.

Andreas Müller: Cool, bye. Thank you.

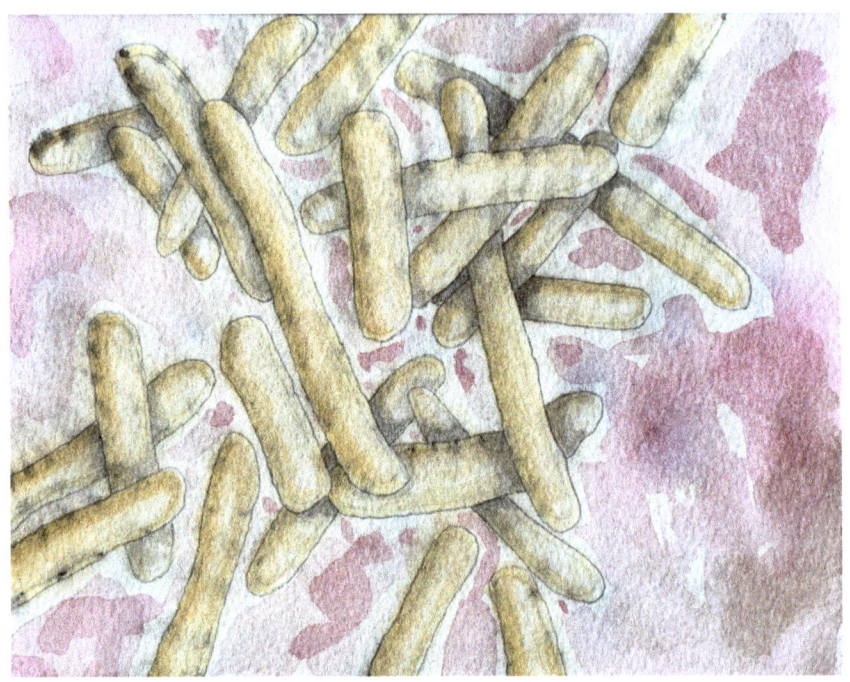

PLACEBO

Justin Allen:	Long time.
Andreas Müller:	Long time, absolutely. Nice to see you.
Justin Allen:	Good to see you too.
Andreas Müller:	So how are you doing?
Justin Allen:	Good. And you?
Andreas Müller:	Yeah, also good.
Justin Allen:	So do you want to just jump into it or do you want to do an intro?
Andreas Müller:	Maybe I do a short introduction if that's fine for you.
Justin Allen:	Yeah.
Andreas Müller:	Yeah. Just, okay, a few more people are joining.
Andreas Müller:	Okay. So, hello everyone. Just to let you know what's going on here, there is Justin and I, we will continue to have our conversations. I don't know if you know it, we published a book in 2020 (*No-Point Perspective*) already with conversations we had on this issue and we just thought we'd go on with those conversations, but now they're open so you can watch it live.

Andreas Müller:	But after checking it out a bit we decided that it's quite okay to not have questions from the audience, so it's just Justin and me who will have the conversation and you are free to watch it and follow it or leave again or anything you want basically. And that's why it's also recorded. Only my picture is recorded, but the idea is maybe, we don't know what happens, it will become a second book or a podcast or something like that, but that's why it's recorded. You won't be seen anyway. And as you don't ask questions, you will also not be heard (laughing). Yeah, I think that was... And just to let you know, I think Justin and I, we haven't spoken since July or August now. And hello Justin.
Justin Allen:	Hello. So I took some notes.
Andreas Müller:	Hmm.
Justin Allen:	But they ended up being only three words and I don't remember why...
Andreas Müller:	All right.
Justin Allen:	...why I wanted to talk about them yet, so we'll have to figure that out, but the three words are placebo... Do you know what a placebo is?
Andreas Müller:	Yeah, the medicine which doesn't have any substance so to speak or yeah, it's not supposed to work but it seems to work or something like that.
Justin Allen:	Right (laughing). And then path was the second one.
Andreas Müller:	All right.
Justin Allen:	And then convincing was the third one. So, placebo, path and convincing.

Andreas Müller:	All right.
Justin Allen:	And <u>placebo</u>, I think I'm clearer on what I meant by that or what I wanted to talk to you about.
Andreas Müller:	Mm.
Justin Allen:	Like you said, a placebo is generally used when they want to test a medicine. They give 50% of the people the medicine and 50% of the people a placebo, which is nothing actually.
Andreas Müller:	Yeah.
Justin Allen:	And then they see the results and it's often the case that the placebo (laughing) does better than the people that get the medicine.
Andreas Müller:	I didn't know that.
Justin Allen:	I read about it recently that they're starting to consider using placebos as a healing medicine because it's so effective. And then I don't know my analogy or the way that I was trying to relate it to this was that you kind of have two groups of people taking two medicines. And the people that are taking the placebo, those people, 50% say, "Wow, I feel better." And 50% say, "I don't feel better." But in both cases, nothing's happening to them. So in each case, even if you're feeling better, it can't (technically) be attributed to the placebo. And if you're feeling worse, it also can't (technically) be attributed to the placebo.
Justin Allen:	What could it be that's causing somebody to feel good or not feel good in the sense when nothing has actually changed for them? And then relating that to this, the way that I try to relate to it is that from your, or not from your message, but from what's talked about here is a similar case in the

sense that there's two groups of people. So there's the people that are claiming that they're there and then there's the group that isn't there (laughing).

Andreas Müller: Yes.

Justin Allen: But in both cases from what you talk about, there's nothing actually ever going on in either case as far as there being somebody.

Andreas Müller: Oh, absolutely. Yes. Right.

Justin Allen: So in each case, something's happening, there's reacting. We could say in your case, you're reacting to things that apparently happen and also other people are reacting to things that apparently happen. And the only subtle difference is that some people think that they're there and that things are happening to them and they're doing things.

Andreas Müller: Exactly, that some things are happening to them and that they are also doing things.

Justin Allen: Right.

Andreas Müller: Yeah.

Justin Allen: But in each case it's really a placebo where there's actually nothing there.

Andreas Müller: Yeah. One could say so, yeah. In the end there isn't even a placebo, so to speak, that's just what apparently happened. That's just what's happening.

Justin Allen: Right. But a placebo is essentially nothing.

Andreas Müller: Yeah. Okay.

Justin Allen: You can say a placebo is a pill, generally it's a sugar

	pill or something like that, but it's really nothing. (In the context of its use and purpose it is nothing)
Andreas Müller:	Yeah. I understand. Yeah.
Justin Allen:	So then the next thing was the <u>path</u>. And I think by path, what I meant was, there's this familiar path in these types of talks generally from your side more so than from the audience's side, but from your side, you can kind of say the wall behind you is... You would say that it is apparently happening.
Andreas Müller:	Kind of. Yeah.
Justin Allen:	And then you would say that your body is apparently happening.
Andreas Müller:	Yes.
Justin Allen:	And that thoughts apparently happen.
Andreas Müller:	Yes.
Justin Allen:	And then emotions apparently happen. So in the sense that's a path of where in this case, we started from something that we generally think of as inanimate and an object, the wall or the computer, and then we went to your body or mind, which we think is an animate object. And then we went into your thoughts and feelings which we generally attribute to getting closer to what "we" essentially are.
Andreas Müller:	To "me," closer to... Yeah, yeah.
Justin Allen:	But from what you talk about in all those cases, they're kind of even, they're just equal, a thought happens, a wall happens, they are the same nothing.

Andreas Müller:	Exactly. Yes. There isn't anything that's closer to "me" or further away, or has more value or less value. Because there is "no me" in the end, but yes.
Justin Allen:	All right. So, but then...
Andreas Müller:	This message really levels everything out.
Justin Allen:	Right. And so in one sense, somebody could interpret that or if you hear that, then maybe a logical conclusion would be to then also say, "Okay, so the only reason why I feel like I'm here or that there's a 'me' here is because thought is happening and that thought is telling me that there's a 'me' or that thought is somehow latched onto to it being actually something and that sense creates the sense of 'me'."
Justin Allen:	And in that case, it's the same as a feeling. So you could also say, "No, I don't have thoughts." I might say "No, it's more of a feeling." Or a third way of saying it is that, "No, I just sense, it's a strong, undeniable sense that I'm here." But in each one of those cases, they're the same from what you're talking about in the sense that it's just, if we take the thought example where there's a thought that says I'm here...
Andreas Müller:	Yes.
Justin Allen:	Then the thought is creating this sense of something being there.
Andreas Müller:	Yeah, I wouldn't say so, actually. I would actually say in order to be able to believe the thought, there must already be something there, sorry, this was not good English, but there already has to be something in order to believe this thought because I would say the thought itself wouldn't create the "me."

Justin Allen:	That's what I was wanting you to say.
Andreas Müller:	Yes.
Justin Allen:	So it's not the thought really that's happening and somehow convincing you that you're there. And it's also not a feeling that's happening that's somehow convincing you that you're there.
Andreas Müller:	Yes.
Justin Allen:	But would you say that it's a happening?
Andreas Müller:	Which one?
Justin Allen:	The "me."
Andreas Müller:	Well, yes and no. That's the funny thing because it never really happens, the "me." There is not within anyone this "me" inside. You don't have a "me" inside, I don't have a "me" inside. No one has a "me" inside them. But for some people there is this claim that they are someone on top, but this claim is kind of energetic. It feels as if there is something inside them, that there is this "me."
Justin Allen:	Yeah.
Andreas Müller:	And then one could say on top it seeks for confirmation in thoughts, in feelings, in emotions. It reflects itself in those things and gets confirmed by that. It solidifies itself, so to speak.
Justin Allen:	So if you had to, staying on this topic then, you would say that the wall is apparently happening?
Andreas Müller:	Yeah, but that's already difficult because it's already a story. It's not really something that I can say.
Justin Allen:	But then would you equate... I guess what I'm trying to do is, can we equate the wall as apparently

happening to a "me" for somebody as apparently happening or is there a difference?

Andreas Müller: Yeah, exactly. I would say there is a difference because, that's the thing, there never is anything happening within us, neither a "me" nor a real, separate "me illusion." In the end, anyone saying I am someone is like the wall, but it's equally empty of any experiencing existence. So even this claim, "I am a me," is as empty as the wall. And that's what I would say one could equate with the wall, bodies, apparent bodies saying, "I am someone. I even feel it." That is like the wall. But as the wall is empty of any inside reality so to speak, regarding consciousness or self-experience, there's actually no such thing within us.

Justin Allen: Yeah. But you know how somebody in a talk with you might say, "I feel like I'm not here," then you would say, "Well, that's what's apparently happening."

Andreas Müller: Yes.

Justin Allen: And that's what I mean... So if I say I'm worried, I'm nervous about my flight and I'm asking you for advice. I'm nervous about my flight and I get really worried about it and I feel like I might crash, you would just say, "Well, that's what's apparently happening over there." And if I say to you, "I'm here, me." Then would you also say that's what's apparently happening?

Andreas Müller: Yes, of course, I would also say that's what's apparently happening, but what I mean is the illusion that you are someone is what's apparently happening. I would in that sense never say, "Ah, there is a 'me' apparently happening." I would say you claiming that, or you putting those words out, that's what apparently happens then.

Justin Allen:

Okay. So, there's a distinction where this kind of thing that seems to be happening to most people where they think that they're there...

Andreas Müller:

That's why one could say that the "me" is the only illusion. That there is a "me" is the only illusion.

Justin Allen:

Not a happening.

Andreas Müller:

No, exactly. It's not a happening. It's not real and unreal, like chairs, walls, thoughts. Exactly. It's not that within some people there is a real "me" within them while for a few people that has dropped.

Justin Allen:

Right. And using your language in a way, there's nothing real or unreal.

Andreas Müller:

Yes.

Justin Allen:

So there's no wall anyways and there's no thoughts anyways.

Andreas Müller:

Yes.

Justin Allen:

But when you're talking in this language, then you still generally will comment to somebody where you'll say, "Your thought that you're having is just what's apparently happening, or you're feeling is just what's apparently happening," or somebody's doing an action like cooking or playing sports, then you'd say, "that's what's apparently happening to you."

Andreas Müller:

Yeah.

Justin Allen:

So I'm just saying that when I hear this, I can imagine coming to a conclusion also where you think, "Just like how thoughts are happening here, just how emotions are happening here and how actions are happening here, a 'me' is happening here."

Andreas Müller:	Yes. I understand. I know how the individual, the person can come to this conclusion, but in the end, it's not what's being said.
Justin Allen:	Yeah. So, there's a difference between the thought that's, I mean, not an actual difference, but in the talk, there's a difference between the thought which is happening or the emotion which is happening.
Andreas Müller:	Yeah.
Justin Allen:	That's different than what you might call the energetic... (sense of me happening)
Andreas Müller:	Yes.
Justin Allen:	...Sense of "me" or whatever.
Andreas Müller:	Exactly. One could say so. Yes. Yeah. Because I wouldn't say that those things are an illusion. I wouldn't say the world is an illusion or thoughts and feelings are an illusion. They are real and unreal. And the only illusion is that they are real things that happen.
Justin Allen:	So happenings are any kind of happening, meaning thought, feeling, wall, action. Those are real and unreal. Those aren't illusions.
Andreas Müller:	Yes. One could say so, yes.
Justin Allen:	Yeah. So those aren't illusions. The only thing that is an illusion in this case is a "me."
Andreas Müller:	Yes, exactly. And actually, this sentence "the 'me' is an illusion," means that it (the "me") doesn't exist at all.
Justin Allen:	Right.

Andreas Müller:	In that sense, it doesn't even exist as an illusion (or a happening or as real or unreal). It's just not there. It never takes, well, nothing takes form really. But as I said, everything is equally empty like the wall.
Justin Allen:	So in that sense, just like if we categorize "me's" and "no me's," (laughing) things happen to "no me's" in the exact same way that things happen to "me's." (laughing)
Andreas Müller:	I know what you mean. Yes, one could say so. Yes. Well, nothing happens to "no me's" (and all there "really" is, is "no me's") of course, that's the story, but I know what you mean.
Justin Allen:	Yeah.
Andreas Müller:	Yeah.
Justin Allen:	And the "me" in this sentence also the "me" isn't a story.
Andreas Müller:	Well, let's go back. Let's put it like this, I'm living in the same world where there are people, where there seem to be governments and countries and rules and taxes to be paid and whereas sometimes there is sunshine and sometimes there's rain. Apparently, I live in the same world as everybody does.
Justin Allen:	Yeah.
Andreas Müller:	Yeah.
Justin Allen:	So then as far as stories go, a story is something that happens also.
Andreas Müller:	Yes, absolutely.
Justin Allen:	And you tell stories and everybody tells stories and you hear stories.

Andreas Müller: Yes.

Justin Allen: But the "me" isn't a story.

Andreas Müller: Well, no, the "me" is not a, well, that there is a "me," this information is a story. I would say, but what you probably mean when there is someone, stories are believed to be the truth. The person doesn't really regard stories as stories. There's always the subtle assumption that they somehow contain the truth, at least possibly.

Justin Allen: But then the story... So if you compare a story to a wall (laughing).

Andreas Müller: Yep. Stories are what apparently happens like the wall is what apparently happens.

Justin Allen: Right. So the story is kind of coming after in a sense, it's not the same, the story isn't the "me," the story is after the "me."

Andreas Müller: Yes. Yeah. Or before.

Justin Allen: Or outside of the "me," let's say.

Andreas Müller: Yeah. It's just what apparently happens. Yeah. Ideas, thoughts, what we speak about, these are stories.

Justin Allen: And then the difference would be, is that if I told a wall a story (laughing), generally the wall wouldn't believe it or it would have no significance in a sense to the wall.

Andreas Müller: Yes.

Justin Allen: And if I told you a story, it would also be possibly entertaining let's say, but what it wouldn't have, is meaning, ever, no matter what story I told you.

Andreas Müller:	Yes, exactly. It would be, in that sense, I'm a human wall. Yes. Yeah. I don't even notice that "someone" is speaking to me. Yeah (laughing). Sorry, it's really a bad thing to say in a conversation. And me reacting to it, and me apparently understanding, is just, I think Tony (Tony Parsons - *The Open Secret*) would probably say this is the wall walling and Andreas is Andreas-ing.
Justin Allen:	Yeah.
Justin Allen:	But you would also say, "Apparently the wall is walling and apparently Andreas is Andreas-ing."
Andreas Müller:	Oh, of course. Yes. That's what apparently happens. Yeah.
Justin Allen:	So I think I understand why I wrote the convincing note too. So in a sense, people that are there, they're convinced that they're there.
Andreas Müller:	Yes.
Justin Allen:	And they're so convinced that no matter what, even if you could, same way that you could prove to me that if you take a hammer and smash it on my hand that I'll get a bruise or I'll bleed or something. So you could prove it by doing it to me.
Justin Allen:	Or you can explain to me how a computer works and you can show me and then I can also do what you told me to do. And then science could also explain to me how taking medicine might cure me and they can explain the process of how it works or how the chemistry works with my body. And so at some point, there's so much information for each one of these scenarios that I am convinced to take the medicine or I'm convinced no, don't hit my hand with the hammer. And I've learned it and I believe it then.

Justin Allen: So I go about saying don't ever hit me with a hammer. If I need to learn a new thing about a computer, I research it. And if I'm going to take medicine, I ask doctors and I might read about it myself. And maybe I can experiment with myself too, like if a doctor says, "Take this food. It'll help you." And so I take the food for a week and I feel like it's helping me, then I'm convinced that it's helped me. And then with this, no matter what in a sense, no matter if there were a way to teach people to not be "me's," or if you could show a spreadsheet and diagrams and real-life scenarios where it was so obvious that people aren't there…

Justin Allen: So same with Santa Claus, you can take children that believe Santa Claus is there (real) for a certain amount of time. Nothing you can say to them generally, even if you come as an adult and you say, "Santa's not real," but it's already been put into their conditioning that Santa's real. They're probably not going to believe you yet.

Andreas Müller: Yet. Maybe not. Yeah.

Justin Allen: And also depends on who's telling the child, but let's just say that in general children believe Santa's there. And then there's a period when they start to maybe doubt and then they transition to realizing Santa's not there. And then to that child that realized Santa's not there, then they become a part of it as parents, where they're the ones putting presents under the Christmas tree. So at that point when the child becomes a parent and is maintaining this illusion to their own kids, to that parent it's so obvious to them that Santa's not real anymore.

Andreas Müller: Yes.

Justin Allen: And I know that if you could do the same thing to a person that's convinced that they're a "me," if you could walk them through it, somehow, if you could take them into the future and show how they're really not there, in this case, the way that you talk about it, they still would not be unconvinced. (They would remain convinced that they are there - that they are experiencing)

Andreas Müller: Mm. Yeah. Because being someone is not really a conviction, I would say. One could say the conviction to be someone, the belief in that thought "I am" as a solidifying element, that's already a symptom of being someone. But being someone isn't really a conviction in that sense. The experience to be someone is the sense of presence. That's what it consists of, so to speak. And then on top, it believes stories about itself. This would be the conviction like, aha, there is the Christmas man, what is it called? Santa Claus. Exactly. There is Santa Claus, and this conviction can be replaced with another conviction or another knowing, "Ah, Santa Claus didn't exist, it was God himself or my parents or whatever that brought the gifts." And in a way, the person can also change the convictions about itself.

Andreas Müller: I'm a human being, but this can be replaced by the conviction, no, actually I'm pure consciousness or I'm a German. No, I'm not a German. I'm a European. Those would all be the convictions to stories about what I am. But the sense of "I am" itself, I would say, isn't a conviction. That's exactly why you can't do anything. You can change the beliefs, kind of, you can change your story, and many people think that's about what life is, to change one's story, to stop identifying with troubling things and to start identifying with a bigger thing, so to speak. But "me" can't be unlearned, so to speak. On the one hand, because it's not real. On the other hand, it's kind of deeper than a conviction. It is the sense to be, the sense of existence is the "me" and I wouldn't call this a conviction.

Justin Allen:	Yeah. But you can see how the same way that almost in a sense that somebody believes without doubt that they're there. In general, the only way that you can create a counter statement is that you say, "It's obvious that there's 'no one' here."
Andreas Müller:	Kind of, yeah. But I think it's rather energetic than on this intellectual level with proof and I show you something and you slowly get it. I think this whole… the energy of this meeting apparently undermines the whole sense of "me." That's why I'm not really into intellectual discussions.
Justin Allen:	No, but I'm just saying that from somebody being there also, it's not an intellectual discussion. They can't really intellectually convince somebody that they're actually there. Nobody can prove that they're there.
Andreas Müller:	Kind of, I know what you mean. Yes. In the end, you're right, it's impossible. It would only be an illusory proof, but usually the proof is you can feel it yourself or you feel yourself.
Justin Allen:	Yeah, like we accept things, but it's still, all those things are 100% stories or beliefs or theories.
Andreas Müller:	You're right. You're totally right. The presence of "I am" can't be proven.
Justin Allen:	Right. But I…
Andreas Müller:	Amazingly, no one notices that all those things that the person takes as a proof for its existence actually don't prove anything. But yes, you're right.
Justin Allen:	Yeah. And that's what I mean too, that even if you could, if there were a way to prove that you really are there or not. So if you're a "me" and somebody showed you the proof, you would be like, "Ah,

yeah. Yeah. I agree." And if you were, in your case, let's say a "no me" and someone proved to you that you are actually there, for you, it'd still be no.

Andreas Müller: (laughing)...Fun. I'm here.

Justin Allen: But it wouldn't convince you or not that you're there to be convinced, but it wouldn't, bring you over or convert you.

Andreas Müller: Probably not. It wouldn't make "me" be reborn again, so to speak (laughing).

Justin Allen: Yeah. And so...

Andreas Müller: In the end, people constantly try to convince me that "I am." In the end, they constantly try to convince me that they are, which basically is the attempt to convince me that "I am." And they address me as if "I am," as if I am something. And in a way that is... an attempt is maybe too strong because it's unconscious. But in the end, that is the constant attempt to convince me, "No, no, the world is real. No, my suffering is real. No, life is about something." And stuff like that. So actually, one could say that happens all the time.

Justin Allen: But if you also could, the same way that if you could prove that actually we are here, there are things inside or whatever, if you could prove that it's actually not the case. So if you could literally prove to people that no, you're not there, it wouldn't convert them or it wouldn't make them disappear or that they would suddenly not be anymore.

Andreas Müller: Yes, exactly. The thing is, on the one hand that, of course, the whole idea of proof needs a certain reality in which there are circumstances that can be proved. So of course, the whole idea of proof is already in the story. Well, the thing is that in the end, it can't be proven because all of it isn't real.

Justin Allen:	Yeah.
Andreas Müller:	And also the illusion to be someone just is what apparently happens for no reason. So you can't switch it on and off.
Justin Allen:	Right. But what I'm saying in a way, I'm just pointing out the dilemma which you've pointed out a thousand times, but I do it in a different way. That's the dilemma that if you and I are the only two people on this planet...
Andreas Müller:	And you are someone and I am not (laughing).
Justin Allen:	Yeah. Or vice versa.
Andreas Müller:	Poor you, poor you (laughing).
Justin Allen:	Our discussion might be... we might spend the whole day with me trying to convince you that you're there and you trying to convince me I'm not there (laughing).
Andreas Müller:	No, no, I wouldn't actually try to convince you.
Justin Allen:	I know, but you would by the nature of the conversation because I might say, "But don't you realize this?" And you would say, "No, I don't realize this. There's 'no one' here to realize it." So, you'd be you reacting to me and I'd be reacting to you.
Andreas Müller:	Yeah. Yeah, you might think I tried to convince you and you would hope that you can convince me to finally have a friend.
Justin Allen:	Yeah. But in both cases, nobody would know. In your case...
Andreas Müller:	Yes. Absolutely.

Justin Allen: You wouldn't know because there's "no one" there to know. In my case, I could never be sure that you're not there. For me you would always be there.

Andreas Müller: Yes. But, so for you. Apparently, there would be the illusion of knowing, at least the theoretical possibility of knowing. It would always dance around those ideas of knowing, or that there is a truth even if you don't know it. There would be doubt, belief and doubt. This would be what you would live in. When there is "no one," so to speak, it just wouldn't matter at all. I don't even know what I would need to know or believe in or not because you are assuming yourself to be someone would be utterly and totally fine for me.

Justin Allen: Yeah.

Andreas Müller: But for the person, there would always be something wrong.

Justin Allen: Well, the person in general would just think that you're, in this case, they might think that you're insane or that you're playing a trick.

Andreas Müller: Yes, exactly.

Justin Allen: Or they might think that you've, in the sense of not necessarily being insane, but that you've just been so convinced the same way that I remember when I was five years old and I was convinced that Santa Claus was the one leaving presents under my Christmas tree. (You, Andreas, are just as convinced that you are not there as I was convinced that Santa Claus was the one giving me presents)

Andreas Müller: Which would be additionally weird if that's the only person you have (laughing). If you're left with the only person where you constantly think, "Well, he's crazy. Fucking hell, he's crazy."

Justin Allen: But either way, there'd never be any way for you to prove that you're not there or that there's "no one" there in the same way that I couldn't prove that I am here and I couldn't convince you that I'm here or change your mind. You couldn't change me. (and I couldn't change you)

Andreas Müller: Yes. You're totally right. Yes. Though, again, the person of course would live in the conviction that it's there and it thinks that it can be. For the person, the idea that it can't really prove its existence, is just conceptual.

Justin Allen: But it doesn't have to. This is what I'm saying in a way, the same way you don't have to prove that you're not there, a "me" doesn't have to (prove that a "me" is here), like generally none of us really have to prove that we're here. It's so obvious that we're here.

Andreas Müller: Yeah, exactly. Absolutely. But this obviousness for the person seems to be the proof. That's what I mean. It's so ordinary. It's so normal to be there. For the person, it's so normal to experience itself. But that's actually a proof, it's just so normal that it seems as if it doesn't have to do it again and again, so to speak.

Justin Allen: Yeah. But because it doesn't have to prove that it's there, it's just there fundamentally.

Andreas Müller: Yeah. Yes and no, because I think this, I'm just there is actually also conceptual because actually it isn't always there. I think that's why people constantly have to do something actually.

Andreas Müller: Almost as if they need to prove to themselves their existence in telling stories, in making contact with others, in being active inside. Because I think for the person also this idea that I'm always there, which some spiritual people try to establish, is I would call this actually a conviction because the "me" isn't there actually, at least even in the story, one could say, it's not always there. I think that's why it actually seems to be quite active and always needs some self-solidification. It's all unconscious. It doesn't do that consciously. But I think it does that in order to feel itself, to prove that it's still there, to know that it's still there and to not get lost on the way. But you're right, it would all be apparent, it wouldn't be real. Nothing of that would be real in the end. But that's the thing, my impression is for the person these are just concepts. And yes, I could never prove non-existence.

Justin Allen: Right. And just like the person can't prove that there is existence.

Andreas Müller: And yeah, in the end, it can't prove that.

Justin Allen: But what you're saying is that it actively is trying to prove that.

Andreas Müller: In the end, yes. Actually, it's constantly trying to prove its existence by being active, by believing stories. But it's artificial because one could say it's gone the moment it doesn't do that anymore. Kind of. Not that it has a choice. It's hard to say, because...

Justin Allen: Where there's a "me" there doing this in a sense.

Andreas Müller: That too is what apparently happens that I would say, it's this whole dynamic, is the "me," so to speak, the sense of presence and then almost instantly the need to solidify itself, to confirm itself.

Justin Allen: Right. But that's where from the beginning of the conversation to this point, if we just put it into the timeline of a human life and we say that the "me" starts at two years old, that isn't a happening.

Andreas Müller:	Yeah. Right.
Justin Allen:	But then after that, illusion, that beginning, I'm going to say beginning, but I'm really calling it an illusion, then there's happenings.
Andreas Müller:	The illusion of happenings.
Justin Allen:	Yeah.
Andreas Müller:	For the person.
Justin Allen:	...within that illusion then from that "me" perspective, then things are happening.
Andreas Müller:	Yes, yes.
Justin Allen:	Yeah. And if that two-year-old didn't somehow begin with the "me," then there would be happenings also, but they wouldn't be happening to this "me."
Andreas Müller:	So to speak, yes.
Justin Allen:	And so in that sense, there's never any happenings for that "no me" because it never even came about in a sense.
Andreas Müller:	Yes. Yes.
Justin Allen:	So then there'd be no story for that "no me" either.
Andreas Müller:	Yes, absolutely. Yeah.
Justin Allen:	So then when there is a "me," then things happen to that "me" and that's when the story is being told of those things that are happening to the "me." And then you would say but the main story is just that "me."
Andreas Müller:	Yes.

Justin Allen:

So that's the main story and then the other things would be the chapters or something like that.

Andreas Müller:

Yeah, exactly. That's the main story that goes through the whole book. Yeah.

Justin Allen:

When you talk about stories in your talks, when you say, "that's in the story," those are just chapters that you're talking about when you say, "that's in the story."?

Andreas Müller:

Yeah.

Justin Allen:

But what's the real story or the kind of, I don't know how to subcategorize all this, but the real story is just the "me."

Andreas Müller:

Well, yes, kind of. Seen from the "me," I am the basis of all other stories. I am the basis of my whole life, so I'm the basis for every experience, that's why some spiritual teachers claim you are the, I don't know how they say, the seed of the world. Because of you everything can happen or something, or underneath every experience, are "you," the experiencer. Yes.

Justin Allen:

If as a "me" in a sense you kind of, for whatever reason start to question your existence, meaning that you start to say, "There's no way I can actually be here." Or let's say that you're a trained scientist and you've done already 20 years of experimenting in science and proving things wrong or not. And you run that same kind of an analysis towards yourself. And you come to the conclusion that you can't prove that you're there, but that wouldn't do anything to that sense or that feeling or that energetic, whatever you want to call it.

Andreas Müller:

Exactly. Not necessarily. Apparently it could, but then for no reason at all. But yes, it wouldn't change your sense of "I am" because all that you find out is still "you" having found something out. And the same happens in spirituality, but I'm sure the same happens in science, that there are people really questioning themselves in neuroscience and that stuff where they found out that they can't find a "me" and they can't prove the existence of a "me." Same in spirituality with people asking themselves for 10 years, "Who am I? Is there someone"? Very easily actually coming to the conclusion that there is no real "I," but somehow they or the "I" having that insight survives this insight.

Justin Allen: Right.

Andreas Müller: And same happens with the scientists, for example. And the scientist, he or she, can look at the paper so to speak and say: "We proved that there is no I."

Justin Allen: Right. They've done that already.

Andreas Müller: Exactly. Like the spiritual seeker says, I've seen a hundred thousand times, a hundred thousand times that actually there is no "I." I've looked inside me, I've really looked for it. And many of them report that they couldn't find it. But still, as there was someone investigating, you end up being someone having a conclusion.

Justin Allen: Yeah. That's what I wanted to talk about in the sense of how I would... Like that original story or that original "me" that seems to happen can never be undone because even now within the past 10 years, neuroscientists or whoever it is that are looking at the brain, they can really prove at least with the logic that we have available to us that you're not there. And they even write books where they're saying it didn't do anything other than make them have more doubt or more belief.

Andreas Müller:	But the funny thing is just when you said it, you said they can really prove in the end that's the illusion, that they can really prove that there is "no one" in a real world. In the end, this too is an apparent proof in an apparent reality.
Justin Allen:	Yeah. Well that's what I wanted to say. It's like - you know *Terminator*?
Andreas Müller:	Yeah.
Justin Allen:	Well, I think it's in *Terminator* where he cuts himself and then he sees the robot underneath him. Or at least they've shown that in some films where, or even the films where there's a robot, what is that film with Harrison Ford?
Andreas Müller:	I haven't seen that one.
Justin Allen:	*Blade Runner*, I think.
Andreas Müller:	Yeah.
Justin Allen:	Well, anyways, in one of those stories where the robots don't even know that they're robots (laughing) so they think that they're just like humans basically.
Andreas Müller:	Perfect.
Justin Allen:	And then somebody cuts them and then they see that they're not organic, let's say.
Andreas Müller:	Yeah, and that puts them into a deep depression (laughing).
Justin Allen:	Yeah. But nobody would be different. Any human right now, like anybody listening to this talk, if they were to cut away their skin and reveal that there's just metal underneath it, that wouldn't change

their sense of being there. It might change their philosophy of life, but…

Andreas Müller: Exactly. It would change their conviction, their story about themselves.

Justin Allen: Right. But it wouldn't change the "self" or it wouldn't change the "me."

Andreas Müller: Exactly. One could say.

Justin Allen: Or it could, but let's just say in general it wouldn't.

Andreas Müller: Yeah. Yes.

Justin Allen: And if it did, if the cutting away of the skin and revealing that there's metal underneath did, let's say seem to make the "me" disappear, you would never say it's because of that.

Andreas Müller: Yes, exactly. It would just be what apparently happens. Yes. Yeah. In a way, the "me" constantly has experiences like that. That was an extreme picture, but in the end, the "me" has to constantly readjust its story about itself and about the world. In the end, almost every moment, it has to invent a new story about itself because it constantly reacts slightly different. There are always new experiences happening for the person. So actually it constantly does do that. And of course, the more its experiences are different from its view of itself (and the world), the more shattering it might be, the revelation who I actually am or how much I would need to rewrite my own story. And for the person, this can cause deep trouble like this, "I thought I'm a human, now it turns out that I'm a robot." Some people might be shocked by that.

Justin Allen: Yeah.

Andreas Müller:	But in small parts, it's happening all the time. I think people would call this identity crisis. "I thought I'm a nice guy, but unfortunately yesterday I killed my partner" or something. "Up to then, I thought I'm in control" or, sorry, it was an extreme (example), but I think stuff like that happens that everybody knows this, I guess.
Justin Allen:	You've been waking up every morning in a sense is having to reconfirm your... (story)
Andreas Müller:	Yeah, exactly, remember your story and to tell, or if something bad happens, people quite quickly need to tell a nice story about themselves, why they do it, why they did it and why it was all right to do it and stuff like that. But as you said, all of that never really changes the actual experience of "I am," not even the most extreme insight, "I'm not, I don't exist actually" does. But as long as this is an insight for someone, it doesn't change the experience to be someone. It just remains another concept or belief, which hopefully can become a conviction. I think some people would even think this is liberation when I finally can convince myself about the fact that I don't exist.
Justin Allen:	Yeah. But that's what is so, I guess that's what I find fascinating is that a scientist, it's the first time that there's technology available and enough information or data gathered where they can actually perform a test, which at least to our understanding of the world and the scientific language that we have and the understanding of consciousness, has already disproved (self) and it doesn't change anything for those people that directly saw it.
Andreas Müller:	Yes. Yes.
Justin Allen:	There's a hundred people or a thousand people that witnessed "nobody" being there.

Andreas Müller:	At least from a scientific angle. But as I say, on a spiritual level, there are hundreds of thousands of people since years who saw that.
Justin Allen:	Yeah.
Andreas Müller:	But still they went on being...
Justin Allen:	But in our understanding at least, it's also for 50,000 years or something, we all believed in God. And now not all of us do. But all of us believe that we're there or are convinced that we're here.
Andreas Müller:	And as a story, actually, I talked about this with someone today, and in the end, who knows, who knows what in 50 or a hundred years? Maybe it's impossible to keep that belief up. And maybe it's even impossible to keep that sense of "I am" up when it's constantly bombarded from all sides with not being there, so to speak. But so far, yeah. I mean, it's still quite new also for scientists.
Justin Allen:	Right. That's why I compare that in a way to the child. There's the three, five-year-old's and somebody comes in and tells them that there's not Santa and shows them the hidden presents in the parents closet and kind of kills the illusion for them. If they don't believe you, you'd be shocked in a way.
Andreas Müller:	Yeah. Understand.
Justin Allen:	Two out of the three still believe, but then you'd at least expect the eldest of the three to then come around and see the light in the sense and go, "Ah, yeah, Santa's dead to me now."
Andreas Müller:	Yeah. Understand. As I say, on the one hand, one could compare it to a certain degree. And on the other hand, one can't compare it at all because it's not about convictions and changing one story.

Justin Allen:

There's a difference, you having this talk and just kind of never giving, in a sense, you're never addressing the "me." But you're not actively convincing anybody that they're not there. And this approach that you are doing doesn't work either in the sense that it's not converting people, and it's the same way a scientist might not have actively been trying to... they're actively trying to prove consciousness or they're actively trying to figure out what it is exactly or what we are exactly. And then even if they're actively trying to find that out and they discover that it's not there, it doesn't change, it doesn't switch something for them... (so far)

Andreas Müller:

Yeah, exactly. Yeah. Their personal life, most likely their experience to be someone will just go on. Somehow now having a new story to tell. It's like for the "me," it feels like additional information, something that one can know on top even to all the knowing. That's how it would seem to the person. I know everything I know and on top, I know now that I don't exist actually.

Justin Allen:

Yeah.

Andreas Müller:

The person hopes that there is some gain in knowing that for itself. That's the hope at least. But that's the funny thing in that sense, even the knowledge, the apparent knowledge of I don't exist confirms one's existence.

Justin Allen:

Yeah.

Andreas Müller:

That's the funny thing, the person would even use this sentence to solidify its existence, to feel great about knowing this very unusual and unexpected fact. "You know what? Actually, we don't even exist. Oh, that's great to know. That's interesting. That's new. That's revolutionary." But it would still confirm themselves to be, and be able to know this sentence.

Justin Allen: That's why you have to, or at least that's why I assume that you use the word energetic.

Andreas Müller: Yes.

Justin Allen: I wish there was a different word.

Andreas Müller: I know. There is absolutely no word for it because it doesn't exist. That's the thing. Every word we would use here would just be purely made up.

Justin Allen: But that's why you have to use the word energetic because it has in a sense, it's a word that has no meaning.

Andreas Müller: Yeah (laughing), exactly.

Justin Allen: And it also means everything at the same time.

Andreas Müller: Yeah. Well, I think what it does, it creates a differentiation between, it's not mental, it's not intellectual, it's not emotional in the sense of "I am," it's not a feeling really like sadness or joy or anger. It's yeah, it's energetic. I don't like it too, but I couldn't come up with another word as well.

Justin Allen: But it's the most appropriate word for now because like you just described it, it's something that you can't quite place your finger on or you can't...

Andreas Müller: Yes.

Justin Allen: Nobody's really knows what energy is, I guess.

Andreas Müller: Yes. In a way I don't say that the "me" is energetic or something. It's actually how it describes itself. It's actually those stories. It's actually the awareness teachings. And actually, in many awareness teachings, they even say you can't know who you are, but you can know that you are. You can experience yourself, but you can't know what you are exactly. So they even play with those concepts.

Justin Allen: Science does also.

Andreas Müller: Yeah, I guess so. Yeah.

Justin Allen: Science (Einstein) I think would say everything's energy. A rock is energy, it's just densely packed matter. And other things are loosely packed of elements or matter (which are also just energy).

Andreas Müller: Yeah. Yep. But the thing is that whole reality doesn't exist. That's what I said before. All those proofs are apparent proofs because this reality isn't real where you can prove if there is a "me" or not. But they only think that now they have proven something that's real in a real world. So it's useless. It doesn't prove anything really because this reality isn't real. Because who would know if there's a "me" or not, it all doesn't make sense really.

Justin Allen: But also either way, whether you have the energetic "me" happening or not, it's no difference.

Andreas Müller: Yes. Both would be what apparently happens and both doesn't know itself.

Justin Allen: And let's say that it could also be true that as humans are apparently having a "me" happening, that inanimate objects like walls could also be having an energetic "me" happening to them.

Andreas Müller: Well, they would be in a very bad place because they wouldn't be able to move at all (laughing).

Justin Allen: That's your perspective, isn't it?

Andreas Müller:	They would just bear their pure presence. No, in the end, it's impossible. Only the "me" would be able to assume that, so to speak.
Justin Allen:	Right. But let's say a "me" is assuming the position of a human or it (could be a rock) ...
Andreas Müller:	Well in a very funny way, it does do that. There are many, sorry I have to come back to that again, esoteric or spiritual movements, which of course think that everything is consciousness and that everything is kind of filled with a spiritual essence so to speak, even the walls and rocks and things. They would actually turn everything into this personal reality. And they do, even so-called material things. They would believe to be alive and to be personal and have their own soul and stuff like that. There are people who try to do that.
Justin Allen:	But, just as it seems to apparently be happening that humans are "me's" or having a "me," it would be as reasonable to assume in this context that a rock, there might be rocks where...
Andreas Müller:	It's all in the story. It's a total story. But of course, seen from the "me," there is some logic to it. Of course. Why not?
Justin Allen:	Yeah.
Andreas Müller:	For the person, everything that is imaginable might also be possible. The person can't really, it's a matter of belief only, but the person can't really discriminate. Everything that it can think of might theoretically be the case.
Justin Allen:	But also, from a "no me" perspective in a sense, there's no difference between if you're talking to somebody that's positive that they're there. Right?
Andreas Müller:	Yeah, but I never think that's a real possibility.

That's the thing. Here, there never is taking it to be possible really. There's just "no one" there even taking it. I don't do anything with stuff like that. In that sense, I never think, could this be possible or not because nothing is possible. In that sense, what we talk about, there is no possibility of anything being really the case.

Justin Allen: Yeah. So for you everybody's just as equally not there as with inanimate objects.

Andreas Müller: So to speak. And when you say for "me," that's already... There's just nothing there which can cope with this whole assumed reality, so to speak. It's not recognized at all. No matter what you think about this reality, could it be this, or could it be more like that, or is this the case, or do you believe that there is absolutely nothing here? I can't even go there so to speak, or there is nothing there even being able to go there and think about, could this be the case or not?

Justin Allen: Right.

Andreas Müller: Does Corona exist or not? Is there someone or not? This whole reality doesn't exist.

Justin Allen: But even that you can't say (laughing).

Andreas Müller: Exactly. Yes, yes. That too isn't a belief that I'm carrying around.

Justin Allen: Yeah. But you say that this is not a reality in a sense as a reaction to the global claim that there is a reality.

Andreas Müller: Yeah. It's not an opposite reality. In saying there is no reality, I'm not claiming an opposite reality.

Justin Allen: Yeah.

Andreas Müller:	Yes. Yeah.
Justin Allen:	I think that's it for me.
Andreas Müller:	All right. Yeah. Lovely to see you.
Justin Allen:	Yeah. Good to see you too.
Andreas Müller:	Yeah. Cool. All right. That's it. There's nothing to get and all those things. I wish you a lovely Christmas time.
Justin Allen:	Oh yeah, you too. Ciao.
Andreas Müller:	Yeah. All right. Thank you. Bye. Have a nice evening and day. Thanks.

Andreas Müller was born and grew up in Southern Germany. After having become a spiritual seeker in his teens, he met Tony Parsons in 2009. Since 2011, Andreas has been holding talks and intensives throughout the world.

Justin Allen is an architect in Berlin, Germany. Justin has a background in philosophy and he is originally from upstate New York.